HOMES OF THE LON

CW01510278

BY

MISS OCTAVIA HILL.

REPRINTED FROM THE "FORTNIGHTLY REVIEW" AND "MACMILLAN'S MAGAZINE,"

BY PERMISSION OF THE AUTHOR

COTTAGE PROPERTY IN LONDON.

November 1, 1866.

THE subject of dwellings for the poor is attracting so much attention, that an account of a small attempt to improve them may be interesting to many readers, especially as the plan adopted is one which has answered pecuniarily, and which, while it might be undertaken by private individuals without much risk, would bring them into close and healthy communication with their hard-working neighbors.

Two years ago I first had an opportunity of carrying out the plan I had long contemplated, that of obtaining possession of houses to be let in weekly tenements to the poor. That the spiritual elevation of a large class depended to a considerable extent on sanitary reform was, I considered proved, but I was equally certain that sanitary improvement itself depended upon educational work among grown-up people; that they must be urged to rouse themselves from the lethargy and indolent habits into which they have fallen, and freed from all that hinders them from doing so. I further believed that any lady who would help them to obtain things, the need of which they felt themselves, and would sympathize with them in their desire for such, would soon find them eager to learn her view of what was best for them; that whether this was so or not, her duty was to keep alive their own best hopes and intentions, which come at rare intervals, but fade too often for want of encouragement. I desired to be in a condition to free a few poor people from the tyranny and influence of a low class of landlords and landladies; from the corrupting effect of continual forced communication with very degraded fellow-lodgers; from the heavy incubus of accumulated dirt: that so the never-dying hope which I find characteristic of the poor might have leave to spring, and with it such energy as might help them to help themselves. I had not great ideas of what must be done for them, my strongest endeavors were to be used to rouse habits of industry and effort, without which they must finally sink—with which they might render themselves independent of me except as a friend and leader. The plan was one which depended on just governing more than on helping. The first point was to secure such power as would enable me to insist on some essential sanitary arrangements.

I laid the plan before Mr. Ruskin, who entered into it most warmly. He at once came forward with all the money necessary, and took the whole risk of the undertaking upon himself. He showed me, however, that it would be far more useful if it could be made to pay; that a working man ought to be able to pay for his own house; that the outlay upon it ought, therefore, to yield a fair percentage on the capital invested. Thus empowered and directed, I purchased three houses in my own immediate neighborhood. They were leasehold, subject to a small ground-rent. The unexpired term of the lease was for fifty-six years; this we purchased for £750. We spent £78 additional in making a large room at the back of my own house, where I could meet the tenants from time to time. The plan has now been in operation about a year and a half; the financial result is that the scheme has paid five per cent. interest on all the capital,[1] has repaid £48 of the capital; sets of two rooms have been let for little more than the rent of one, the houses have been kept in repair, all expenses have been met for taxes, ground-rent, and insurance. In this case there is no expense for collecting rents, as I do it myself, finding it most important work; but in all the estimates I put aside the usual percentage for it, in case hereafter I may require help, and also to prove practically that it can be afforded in other cases. It should be observed that well-built houses were chosen, but they were in a dreadful state of dirt and neglect. The repairs required were mainly of a superficial and slight character: slight in regard to expense—vital as to health and comfort. The place swarmed with vermin; the papers, black with dirt, hung in long strips from the walls; the drains were stopped, the water supply out of order. All these things were put in order, but no new appliances of any kind were added, as we had determined that our tenants should wait for these until they had proved themselves capable of taking care of them. A regular sum is set aside for repairs, and this is equally divided between the three houses; if any of it remains, after breakage and damage have been repaired, at the end of the quarter, each tenant decides in turn in what way the surplus shall be spent, so as to add to the comfort of the house. This plan has worked admirably; the loss from carelessness has decreased to an amazing extent, and the lodgers prize the little comforts which they have waited for, and seem in a measure to have earned by their care, much more than those bought with more lavish expenditure. The bad debts during the whole time that the plan has been in operation have only amounted to £2 11s. 3d. Extreme punctuality and diligence in collecting rents, and a strict determination that they shall be paid regularly, have accomplished this; as a proof of which it is curious to observe that £1 3s. 3d. of the bad debts, accumulated during two months that I was away in the country. I have tried to remember, when it seemed hardest that the fulfillment of their duties was the best education for the tenants in every way. It has given them a dignity and glad feeling of honorable behavior which has much more than compensated for the apparent harshness of the rule.

Nothing has impressed me more than the people's perception of an underlying current of sympathy through all dealings that have seemed harsh. Somehow, love and care have made themselves felt. It is also wonderful that they should prize as they do the evenness of the law that is over them. They are accustomed to alternate violence of passion and toleration of vice. They expected a greater toleration, ignorant indulgence, and frequent almsgiving; but in spite of this have recognized as a blessing a rule which is very strict, but the demands of which they know, and a government that is true in word and deed. The plan of substituting a lady for a resident landlady of the same class as her tenants is not wholly gain. The lady will probably have subtler sympathy and clearer comprehension of their needs, but she cannot give the same minute supervision that a resident landlady can. Unhappily, the advantage of such a change is, however, at present unquestionable. The influence of the majority of the lower class of people who sub-let to the poor is almost wholly injurious. That tenants should be given up to the dominion of those whose word is given and broken almost as a matter of course, whose habits and standards are very low, whose passions are violent, who have neither large hope nor clear sight, nor even sympathy, is very sad. It seems to me that a greater power is in the hands of landlords and landladies than of school-teachers—power either of life or death, physical and spiritual. It is not an unimportant question who shall wield it. There are dreadful instances in which sin is really tolerated and shared; where the lodger who will drink most with his landlord is most favored, and many a debt overlooked, to compensate for which the price of rooms is raised; and thus the steady and sober pay more rent to make up for losses caused by the unprincipled. But take this as an example of entirely careless rule: The owner of some cottage property in London, a small undertaker by trade, living some little distance from his property, and for the most part confining his dealings with it to a somewhat fruitless endeavor to collect the rents on a Sunday morning, in discussing the value of the property with me, said very straightforwardly, "Yes, miss; of course there are plenty of bad debts. It's not the rents I look to, but the deaths I get out of the houses." The man didn't mean for a moment that he knew that the state of the houses brought him a plentiful harvest of deaths, though I knew it, and heard the truth ringing with awful irony through his words; but he did mean that his entire thought was of his profits—that those dependent souls and bodies were to him as nothing. Consider under such a rule what deadly quarrels spring up and deepen and widen between families compelled to live very near one another, to use many things in common, whose uneducated minds brood over and over the same slight offenses, when there is no one either compulsorily to separate them, or to say some soothing word of reconciliation before the quarrel grows too serious. I have received a letter from an Irish tenant actually boasting that he "would have taken a more manly way of settling a dispute," but that his neighbor "showed the white feather and retired." I have seen that man's whole face light up and break into a smile when I suggested that a little willing kindness would be a more manly way still. And I have known him and his aunt, though boiling over with rage all the time, use steady self-control in not quarreling for a whole month, because they knew it would spoil my holiday! Finally, they shook hands and made peace, and lived in peace many months, and, indeed, are living so now.

I could have formed no idea of the docility of the people, nor of their gratitude for small things. They are easily governed by firmness, which they respect much. I have always made a point of carefully recognizing their own rights; but if a strong conviction is clearly expressed they readily adopt it, and they often accept a different idea from any they have previously desired, if it is set before them. One tenant—a silent, strong, uncringing woman, living with her seven children and her husband in one room—was certain "there were many things she could get for the children to eat which would do them more good than another room." I was perfectly silent. A half-pleading, half-asserting voice said: "Don't you see I'm right, miss?" "No," I said; "indeed I do not. I have been brought up to know the value of abundant good air, but of course you must do as you think best—only I am sorry." Not a word more passed; but in a few weeks a second room was again to let, and the woman volunteered: "She thought she'd better strive to get the rent; good air was very important, wasn't it?" Again: a man wouldn't send his children to school. Dirty, neglected, and unhappy, they destroyed many things in the house. I urged, to no purpose, that they should be sent. At last I gave him notice to leave because he refused to send them, and because he had taken three children to sleep in the room I had let for his own family only. The man was both angry and obstinate. I quietly went on with proceedings for getting rid of him. He knew I meant what I said, and he requested an interview. He owed no rent, he urged. "No," I replied, "you know what a point I make of that; but it isn't quite the only thing I insist on. I cannot allow anything so wrong as this neglect of the children and overcrowding to continue where I have the power to prevent it." He "knew what it was just this year to fuss about the cholera, and then nobody 'd care how many slep in a room; but he wasn't a coward to be frightened at the cholera, not he! And as to being bound, he wouldn't be bound—no, not to his own master that paid him wage; and it wasn't likely he would to me, when he paid rent reg'lar. The room was his; he took it, and if he paid rent he could do as he liked in it." "Very well," I said; "and the house is mine; I take it, and I must do what I think right in it; and I say that most landladies won't take in children at all, and we all know it is a good deal of loss and trouble; but I'll risk these gladly if you will do what you can to teach the children to be good, and careful, and industrious; and if not, you know the rule, and you must go. If you prefer liberty, and dirt, and mess, take them; but if you choose to agree to live under as good a rule as I can make it, you can stay. You have your choice." Put in the light of a bargain, the man was willing enough. Well, he'd not "do anything contrairy, without telling me, about lodgers; and as to the children, he thought he could turn himself, and send them a bit, now his work was better."

With the great want of rooms there is in this neighborhood it did not seem right to expel families, however large, inhabiting one room. Whenever from any cause a room was vacant, and a large family occupied an adjoining one, I have endeavored to induce them to rent the two. To incoming tenants I do not let what seems decidedly insufficient accommodation. We have been able to let two rooms for four shillings and sixpence, whereas the tenants were in many cases paying four shillings for one. At first they considered it quite an unnecessary expenditure to pay more rent for a second room, however small the additional sum might be. They have gradually learnt to feel the comfort of having two rooms, and pay willingly for them.[2]

The pecuniary success of the plan has been due to two causes. First, to the absence of middlemen; and secondly, to great strictness about punctual payment of rent. At this moment not one tenant in any of the houses owes any rent, and during the whole time, as I have said, the bad debts have been exceedingly small. The law respecting such tenancies seems very simple, and when once the method of proceeding is understood, the whole business is easily managed; and I must say most seriously that I believe it to be better to pay legal expenses for getting rid of tenants than to lose by arrears of rent,—better for the whole tone of the households, kinder to the tenants. The rule should be clearly understood, and the people will respect themselves for having obeyed it. The commencement of proceedings which are known to be genuine and not a mere threat is usually sufficient to obtain payment of arrears: in one case only has an ejectment for rent been necessary. The great want of rooms gives the possessors of such property immense power over their lodgers. Let them see to it that they use it righteously. The fluctuations of work cause to respectable tenants the main difficulties in paying their rent. I have tried to help them in two ways. First, by inducing them to save: this they have done steadily, and each autumn has found them with a small fund accumulated, which has enabled them to meet the difficulties of the time when families are out of town. In the second place, I have done what I could to employ my tenants in slack seasons. I carefully set aside any work they can do for times of scarcity, and I try so to equalize in this small circle the irregularity of work, which must be more or less pernicious, and which the childishness of the poor makes doubly so. They have strangely little power of looking forward; a result is to them as nothing if it will not be perceptible till next quarter! This is very curious to me, especially as seen in connection with that large hope to which I have alluded, and which often makes me think that if I could I would carve over the houses the motto, "Spem, etiam illi habent, quibus nihil aliud restat."

Another beautiful trait in their character is their trust; it has been quite marvelous to find how great and how ready this is. In no single case have I met with suspicion or with anything but entire confidence.

It is needless to say that there have been many minor difficulties and disappointments. Each separate person, who has failed to rise and meet the help that would have been so gladly given has been a distinct loss to me; for somehow the sense of relation to them has been a very real one, and a feeling of interest and responsibility has been very strong even where there was least that was lovely or lovable in the particular character. When they have not had sufficient energy or self-control to choose the sometimes hard path that has seemed the only right one, it would have been hard to part from them, except for a hope that others would be able to lead them where I have failed.

Two distinct kinds of work depend entirely on one another if they are to bear their full fruit. There is, firstly, the simple fulfillment of a landlady's bounden duties, and uniform demand of the fulfillment of those of the tenants. We have felt ourselves bound by laws which must be obeyed, however hard obedience might often be. Then, secondly, there is the individual friendship which has grown up from intimate knowledge, and from a sense of dependence and protection. Such knowledge gives power to see the real position of families; to suggest in time the inevitable result of certain habits; to urge such measures as shall secure the education of the children and their establishment in life; to keep alive the germs of energy; to waken the gentler thought; to refuse resolutely to give any help but such as rouses self-help; to cherish the smallest lingering gleam of self-respect; and, finally, to be near with strong help should the hour of trial fall suddenly and heavily, and to give it with the hand and heart of a real old friend, who has filled many relations besides that of almsgiver, who has long ago given far more than material help, and has thus earned the right to give this lesser help even to the most independent spirits.

The relation will finally depend on the human spirits that enter into it; like all others, it may be pernicious or helpful. It is simply a large field of labor where the laborers are few. It has this advantage over many beneficent works—that it calls out a sense of duty, and demands energetic right-doing among the poor themselves, and so purifies and stimulates them.

If any of my poorer friends chance to see this, I hope they will not think I have spoken too exclusively of what we can do for them. I have dwelt on this side of the question because it is the one we are mainly bound to consider; it is for them to think how they can help us. But I must add in gratitude that I have much to thank them for. Their energy and hope amid overwhelming difficulties have made me ashamed of my own laziness and despair. I have seen the inevitable result of faults and omissions of mine that I had never sufficiently weighed. Their patience and thankfulness are a glad cause of admiration to me continually. I trust that our relation to one another may grow better and nearer for many years.

1. It should be remembered that 5 per cent. interest in England on house property, is equivalent to at least 8 per cent. in the United States.—Ed.

2. It is not possible to form any comparison between the rent of rooms in London and New York, the circumstances of the two cities being so different; but the point to be observed is that by a very small increase of rent the amount of accommodation may be doubled.

ORGANIZED WORK AMONG THE POOR.

SUGGESTIONS FOUNDED ON FOUR YEARS' MANAGEMENT
OF A LONDON COURT.

July, 1869.

FURTHER organization in our mode of dealing with the poor is now generally agreed to be necessary, but there is another truth less dwelt upon, yet on the due recognition of which success equally depends. I feel most deeply that the disciplining of our immense poor population must be effected by individual influence; and that this power can change it from a mob of paupers and semi-paupers into a body of self-dependent workers. It is my opinion, further, that although such influence may be brought to bear upon them in very various ways, it may be exercised in a very remarkable manner by persons undertaking the oversight and management of such houses as the poor habitually lodge in. In support of this opinion I subjoin an account of what has been actually achieved in two very poor courts in London.

About four years ago I was put in possession of three houses in one of the worst courts of Marylebone. Six other houses were bought subsequently. All were crowded with inmates. The first thing to be done was to put them in decent tenantable order. The set last purchased was a row of cottages facing a bit of desolate ground, occupied with wretched, dilapidated cow-sheds, manure heaps, old timber, and rubbish of every description. The houses were in a most deplorable condition: the plaster was dropping from the walls: on one staircase a pail was placed to catch the rain that fell through the roof. All the staircases were perfectly dark; the banisters were gone, having been burnt as firewood by tenants. The grates, with large holes in them, were falling forward into the rooms. The washhouse, full of lumber belonging to the landlord, was locked up; thus the inhabitants had to wash clothes, as well as to cook, eat, and sleep, in their small rooms. The dust-bin, standing in the front of the houses, was accessible to the whole neighborhood, and boys often dragged from it quantities of unseemly objects, and spread them over the court. The state of the drainage was in keeping with everything else. The pavement of the back-yard was all broken up, and great puddles stood in it, so that the damp crept up the outer walls. One large but dirty water-butt received the water laid on for the houses: it leaked, and for such as did not fill their jugs when the water came in, or who had no jugs to fill, there was no water. The former landlord's reply to one of the tenants who asked him to have an iron hoop put round the butt to prevent leakage, was, that "if he didn't like it" (*i. e.* things as they were) "he might leave." The man to whom this was spoken—by far the best tenant in the place—is now with us, and often gives his spare time to making his room more comfortable, knowing that he will be retained if he behaves well.

This landlord was a tradesman in a small way of business—not a cruel man, except in so far as variableness of dealing is cruelty; but he was a man without capital to spend on improvements, and lost an immense percentage of his rent by bad debts. I went over the houses with him the last day he collected his rents there, that he might introduce me to the people as the owner of the property. He took a man with him, whom, as he confided to me, he wished to pass off upon the people as a broker.[1] It was evident that, whether they saw through this deceit or not, they had no experience which led them to believe he intended to carry into effect the threats he uttered. The arrears of rent were enormous. I had been informed that the honest habitually pay for the dishonest, the owner relying upon their payments to compensate for all losses; but I was amazed to find to what an extent this was the case. Six, seven, or eight weeks' rent were due from most tenants, and in some cases very much more; whereas, since I took possession of the houses (of which I collect the rents each week myself) I have *never* allowed a second week's rent to become due.

I think no one who has not experienced it can fully realize the almost awed sense of joy with which one enters upon such a possession as that above described, conscious of having the power to set it, even partially, in order. Hopes, indeed, there are which one dare scarcely hope; but at once one has power to say, "Break out a window there in that dark corner; let God's light and air in;" or, "Trap that foul drain, and shut the poisonous miasma, out;" and one has moral power to say, by deeds which speak louder than words, "Where God gives me authority, this, which you in your own hearts know to be wrong, shall not go on. I would not set my conviction, however strong it might be, against your judgment of right; but when you are doing what I know your own conscience condemns, I, now that I have the power, will enforce right; but first I will try whether I cannot *lead* you, yourselves, to arise and cast out the sin— helping your wavering and sorely tried will by mine, which is untempted."

As soon as I entered into possession, each family had an opportunity offered of doing better: those who would not pay, or who led clearly immoral lives, were ejected. The rooms they vacated were cleansed; the tenants who showed signs of improvement moved into them, and thus, in turn, an opportunity was obtained for having each room distempered and painted. The drains were put in order, a large slate cistern was fixed, the wash-house was cleared of its lumber, and thrown open on stated days to each tenant in turn. The roof, the plaster, the woodwork were repaired; the staircase-walls were distempered; new grates were fixed; the layers of paper and rag (black with age) were torn from the windows, and glass was put in; out of 192 panes, only 8 were found unbroken. The yard and footpath were paved.

The rooms, as a rule, were re-let at the same prices at which they had been let before; but tenants with large families were counseled to take two rooms, and for these much less was charged than if let singly: this plan I continue to pursue. In-coming tenants are not allowed to take a decidedly insufficient quantity of room, and no sub-letting is permitted. The elder girls are employed three times a week in scrubbing the passages in the houses, for the cleaning of which the landlady is responsible. For this work they are paid, and by it they learn habits of cleanliness. It is, of course, within the authority of the landlady also to insist on cleanliness of wash-houses, yards, staircases, and staircase-windows; and even to remonstrate concerning the rooms themselves if they are habitually dirty.

The pecuniary result has been very satisfactory. Five per cent. interest has been paid on all the capital invested. A fund for the repayment of capital is accumulating. A liberal allowance has been made for repairs; and here I may speak of the means adopted for making the tenants careful about breakage and waste. The sum allowed yearly for repairs is fixed for each house, and if it has not all been spent in restoring and replacing, the surplus is used for providing such additional appliances as the tenants themselves desire. It is therefore to their interest to keep the expenditure for repairs as low as possible; and instead of committing the wanton damage common among tenants of their class, they are careful to avoid injury, and very helpful in finding economical methods of restoring what is broken or worn out, often doing little repairs of their own accord.

From the proceeds of the rent, also, interest has been paid on the capital spent in building a large room where the tenants can assemble. Classes are held there—for boys, twice weekly; for girls, once; a singing class has just been established. A large work-class for married women and elder girls meets once a week. A glad sight it is—the large room filled with the eager, merry faces of the girls, from which those of the older, careworn women catch a reflected light. It is a good time for quiet talk with them as we work, and many a neighborly feeling is called out among the women as they sit together on the same bench, lend one another cotton or needles, are served by the same hand, and look to the same person for direction. The babies are a great bond of union; I have known the very women who not long before had been literally fighting, sit at the work-class busily and earnestly comparing notes of their babies' respective history. That a consciousness of corporate life is developed in them is shown by the not infrequent use of the expression "One of us."

Among the arrangements conducive to comfort and health I may mention, that instead of the clothes being hung as formerly out of front windows down against the wall, where they could not be properly purified, the piece of ground in front of the houses is used as a drying-ground during school hours. The same place is appropriated as a playground, not only for my younger tenants, but for the children from the neighboring courts. It is a space walled round, where they can play in safety. Hitherto, games at trap, bat and ball, swinging, skipping, and singing a few Kinder-Garten songs with movements in unison, have been the main diversions. But I have just established drill for the boys, and a drum and fife band. Unhappily, the mere business connected with the working of the houses has occupied so much time, that the playground has been somewhat neglected; yet it is a most important part of the work. The evils of the streets and courts are too evident to need explanation. In the playground are gathered together children habitually dirty, quarrelsome, and violent. They come wholly ignorant of games, and have hardly self-control enough to play at any which have an object or require effort. Mere senseless, endless repetition is at best their diversion. Often the games are only repetitions of questionable sentences. For instance, what is to be said of a game the whole of which consists in singing: "Here comes my father all down the hill, all down the hill," (over and over again) and replying, "We won't get up for his ugly face—ugly face" (repeated *ad libitum*)? Then come the mother, the sister, the brother, to whom the same words are addressed. Finally, the lover comes, to whom the greeting is, "We will get up for his pretty face." This was, perhaps, the best game the children knew, yet, in as far as it had any meaning or influence, it must be bad. Compare it, or the wild, lawless fighting or gambling, with a game at trap, arranged with ordered companions, definite object, and progressive skill. The moral influence depends, however, on having ladies who will go to the playground, teach games, act as umpires, know and care for the children. These I hope to find more and more. Until now, except at rare intervals, the playground has been mainly useful for the fresh air it affords to the children who are huddled together by night in small rooms, in the surrounding courts. The more respectable parents keep them indoors, even in the day-time, after school-hours, to prevent their meeting with bad companions.

Mr. Ruskin, to whom the whole undertaking owes its existence, has had trees planted in the playground, and creepers against the houses. In May, we have a May-pole or a throne covered with flowers for the May-queen and her attendants. The sweet luxuriance of the spring-flowers is more enjoyed in that court than would readily be believed. Some months after the first festival the children were seen sticking a few faded flowers into a crevice in the wall, saying, they wanted to make it "like it was the day we had the May-pole."

I have tried, as far as opportunity has permitted, to develop the love of beauty among my tenants. The poor of London need joy and beauty in their lives. There is no more true and eternal law to be recognized about them than that which Mr. Dickens shows in "Hard Times"—the fact that every man has an imagination which needs development and satisfaction. Mr. Slearey's speech, "People mutht be amoothed, Thquire," is often recalled to my mind in dealing with the poor. They work hard; their lives are monotonous; they seek low places of amusement; they break out into lawless "sprees." Almost all amusements—singing, dancing, acting, expeditions into the country, eating and drinking—are liable to abuse; no rules are subtle enough to prevent their leading to harm. But if a lady can know the individuals, and ask them as her invited guests to any of these, an innate sense of honor and respect preserves the tone through the whole company. Indeed, there can hardly be a more proudly thankful moment than that, when we see these many people to whom life is dull and full of anxiety, gathered together around us for holy, happy Christmas festivities, or going out to some fair and quiet spot in the bright summer time, bound to one another by the sense of common relationship, preserved unconsciously from wrong by the presence of those whom they love and who love them. Such intervals of bright joy are easily arranged by friends for friends; but if strangers are invited *en masse*, it is difficult to keep any of these recreations innocent.

All these ways of meeting are invaluable as binding us together; still, they would avail little were it not for the work by which we are connected—for the individual care each member of the little circle receives. Week by week, when the rents are collected, an opportunity of seeing each family separately occurs. There are a multitude of matters to attend to: first, there is the mere outside business—rent to be received, requests from the tenant respecting repairs to be considered: sometimes decisions touching the behavior of other tenants to be made, sometimes rebukes for untidiness to be administered. Then come the sad or joyful remarks about health or work, the little histories of the week. Sometimes grave questions arise about important changes in the life of the family—shall a daughter go to service? or shall the sick child be sent to a hospital? etc.

Sometimes violent quarrels must be allayed. Much may be done in this way, so ready is the response in these affectionate natures to those whom they trust and love. For instance: two women among my tenants fought; one received a dreadful kick, the other had hair torn from her head. They were parted by a lad who lived in the house. The women occupied adjoining rooms, they met in the passages, they used the same yard and wash-house, endless were the opportunities of collision while they were engaged with each other. For ten days I saw them repeatedly: I could in no way reconcile them—words of rage and recrimination were all that they uttered; while the hair, which had been carefully preserved by the victim, was continually exhibited to me as a sufficient justification for lasting anger. One was a cold, hard, self-satisfied, well-to-do woman; the other a nervous, affectionate, passionate, very poor Irishwoman. Now it happened that in speaking to the latter one evening, I mentioned my own grief at the quarrel: a look of extreme pain came over her face; it was a new idea to her that I should care. That, and no sense of the wrong of indulging an evil passion, touched her. The warm-hearted creature at once promised to shake hands with her adversary; but she had already taken out a summons against the other for assault, and did not consider she could afford to make up the quarrel, because it implied losing the two shillings the summons had cost. I told her the loss was a mere nothing to her if weighed in the balance with peace, but that I would willingly pay it. It only needed that one of the combatants should make the first step towards reconciliation for the other (who, indeed, rather dreaded answering the summons) to meet her half-way. They are good neighbors now of some months' standing. A little speech which shows the character of the Irishwoman is worth recording. Acknowledging to me that she was very passionate, she said: "My husband never takes my part when I'm in my tanthrums, and I'm that mad with him; but, bless you, I love him all the better afterwards; he knows well enough it would only make me worse." I may here observe that the above-mentioned two shillings is the only money I ever had to give to either woman. It is on such infinitesimally small actions that the success of the whole work rests.

My tenants are mostly of a class far below that of mechanics. They are, indeed, of the very poor. And yet, although the gifts they have received have been next to nothing, none of the families who have passed under my care during the whole four years have continued in what is called "distress," except such as have been unwilling to exert themselves. Those who will not exert the necessary self-control cannot avail themselves of the means of livelihood held out to them. But, for those who are willing, some small assistance in the form of work has, from time to time, been provided—not much, but sufficient to keep them from want or despair. The following will serve as an instance of the sort of help given, and its proportion to the results.

Alice, a single woman, of perhaps fifty-five years, lodged with a man and his wife—the three in one room—just before I obtained full possession of the houses. Alice, not being able to pay her rent, was turned into the street, where Mrs. S. (my playground superintendent) met her, crying dreadfully.

It was Saturday, and I had left town till Monday. Alice had neither furniture to pawn, nor friends to help her; the workhouse alone lay before her. Mrs. S. knew that I esteemed her as a sober, respectable, industrious woman, and therefore she ventured to express to Alice's landlord the belief that I would not let him lose money if he would let her go back to her lodging till Monday, when I should return home, thus risking for me a possible loss of fourpence—not very ruinous to me, and a sum not impossible for Alice to repay in the future.

I gave Alice two days' needlework, then found her employment in tending a bed-ridden cottager in the country, whose daughter (in service) paid for the nursing. Five weeks she was there, working and saving her money. On her return I lent her what more she required to buy furniture, and she then took a little room direct from me. Too blind to do much household work, but able to sew almost mechanically, she just earns her daily bread by making sailors' shirts! but her little home is her own, and she loves it dearly; and, having tided over that time of trial, Alice can live—has paid all her debts, too, and is more grateful than she would have been for many gifts.

At one time I had a room to let which was ninepence a week cheaper than the one she occupied. I proposed to her to take it; it had, however, a different aspect, getting less of the southern and western sunlight. Alice hesitated long, and asked *me* to decide, which I declined to do; for, as I told her, her moving would suit my arrangements rather better. She, hearing that, wished to move; but I begged her to make her decision wholly irrespective of my plans. At last she said, very wistfully: "Well, you see, miss, it's between ninepence and the sun." Sadly enough, ninepence had to outweigh the sun.

My tenants are, of course, encouraged to save their money. It should, however, be remarked, that I have never succeeded in getting them to save for old age. The utmost I have achieved is that they lay by sufficient either to pay rent in times of scarcity, to provide clothes for girls going to service, or boots, or furniture, or even to avail themselves of opportunities of advancement which must be closed to them if they had not a little reserve fund to meet expenses of the change.

One great advantage arising from the management of the houses is, that they form a test-place, in which people may prove themselves worthy of higher situations. Not a few of the tenants have been persons who had sunk below the stratum where once they were known, and some of these, simply by proving their character, have been enabled to regain their former stations. One man, twenty years ago, had been a gentleman's servant, had saved money, gone into business, married, failed, and then found himself out of the groove of work. When I made his acquaintance he was earning a miserable pittance for his wife and seven unhealthy children, and all the nine souls were suffering and sinking unknown. After watching and proving him for three years I was able to recommend him to a gentleman in the country, where now the whole family are profiting by having six rooms instead of one, fresh air, and regular wages.

But it is far easier to be helpful than to have patience and self-control sufficient, when the times come, for seeing suffering and not relieving it. And yet the main tone of action must be severe. There is much of rebuke and repression needed, although a deep and silent under-current of sympathy and pity may flow beneath. If the rent is not ready, notice to quit must be served. The money is then almost always paid, when the notice is, of course, withdrawn. Besides this inexorable demand for rent (never to be relaxed without entailing cumulative evil on the defaulter, and setting a bad example, too readily followed by others) there must be a perpetual crusade carried on against small evils—very wearing sometimes. It is necessary to believe that in thus setting in order certain spots on God's earth, still more in presenting to a few of His children a somewhat higher standard of right, we are doing His work, and that he will not permit us to lose sight of His large laws, but will rather make them evident to us through the small details.

The resolution to watch pain which cannot be radically relieved except by the sufferer himself is most difficult to maintain. Yet it is wholly necessary in certain cases not to help. Where a man persistently refuses to exert himself, external help is worse than useless. By withholding gifts we say to him in action more mournful than words: "You will not do better. I was ready—I will be ready whenever you come to yourself; but until then you must pursue your own course." This attitude has often to be taken; but it usually proves a summons to a more energetic spirit, producing nobler effort in great matters, just as the notice to quit arouses resolution and self-denial in pecuniary concerns.

Coming together so much as we do for business with mutual duties, for recreation with common joy, each separate want or fault having been dealt with as it arose, it will be readily understood that in such a crisis as that which periodically occurs in the East End of London, instead of being unprepared, I feel myself somewhat like an officer at the head of a well-controlled little regiment, or, more accurately, like a country proprietor with a moderate number of well-ordered tenants.

For, firstly, my people are numbered; not merely counted, but known, man, woman, and child. I have seen their self-denying efforts to pay rent in time of trouble, or their reckless extravagance in seasons of abundance; their patient labor, or their failure to use the self-control necessary to the performance of the more remunerative kinds of work; their efforts to keep their children at school, or their selfish, lazy way of living on their children's earnings. Could any one, going suddenly among even so small a number as these thirty-four families—however much penetration and zeal he might possess—know so accurately as I what kind of assistance would be really helpful, and not corrupting? And if positive gifts must be resorted to, who can give them with so little pain to the proud spirit, so little risk of undermining the feeble one, as the friend of old standing?—the friend, moreover, who has rigorously exacted the fulfillment of their duty in punctual payment of rent; towards whom, therefore, they might feel that they had done what they could while strength lasted, and need not surely be ashamed to receive a little bread in time of terrible want?

But it ought hardly ever to come to an actual doling out of bread or alms of any kind. During the winter of 1867–68, while the newspapers were ringing with appeals in consequence of the distress prevalent in the metropolis, being on the Continent, and unable to organize more satisfactory schemes of assistance, I wrote to the ladies who were superintending the houses for me, to suggest that a small fund (which had accumulated from the rents, after defraying expenses and paying interest) should be distributed in gifts to any of the families who might be in great poverty. The answer was that there were none requiring such help. Now, how did this come to pass?

Simply through the operation of the various influences above described. The tenants never having been allowed to involve themselves in debt for rent (now and then being supplied with employment to enable them to pay it), they were free from one of the greatest drags upon a poor family, and had, moreover, in times of prosperity been able really to save. It is but too often the case that, even when prosperous times come, working people cannot lay by, because then they have to pay off arrears of rent. The elder girls, too, were either in service or quite ready to go; and so steady, tidy, and respectable as to be able to fill good situations. This was owing, in many cases, to a word or two spoken long before, urging their longer attendance at school, or to their having had a few happy and innocent amusements provided for them, which had satisfied their natural craving for recreation, and had prevented their breaking loose in search of it. Health had been secured by an abundance of air, light, and water. Even among this very lowest class of people, I had found individuals whom I could draft from my lodging-houses into resident situations (transplanting them thus at once into a higher grade), simply because I was able to say, "I know them to be honest, I know them to be clean." Think of what this mere fact of *being known* is to the poor!

You may say, perhaps, "This is very well as far as you and your small knot of tenants are concerned, but how does it help us to deal with the vast masses of poor in our great towns?" I reply, "Are not the great masses made up of many small knots? Are not the great towns divisible into small districts? Are there not people who would gladly come forward to undertake the systematic supervision of some house or houses, if they could get authority from the owner? And why should there not be some way of registering such supervision, so that, bit by bit, as more volunteers should come forward, the whole metropolis might be mapped out, all the blocks fitting in like little bits of mosaic to form one connected whole?"

The success of the plan does not depend entirely upon the houses being the property of the superintendent. I would urge people, if possible, to purchase the houses of which they undertake the charge; but if they cannot, they may yet do a valuable little bit of work by registering a distinct declaration that they will supervise such and such a house, or row, or street; that if they have to relinquish the work, they will say so; that if it becomes too much for them, they will ask for help; that any one desiring information about the families dwelling in the houses they manage may apply to them.

It is well known that the societies at work among the poor are so numerous, and labor so independently of each other, that, at present, many sets of people may administer relief to a given family in one day, and perhaps not one go near them again for a long interval; yet each society may be quite systematic in its own field of operation. It seems to me, that though each society might like to go its own way (and, perhaps, to supply wants which the house-overseer might think it best to leave unsupplied), they might at least feel it an advantage to know of a recognized authority, from whom particulars could be learned respecting relief already given, and the history of the families in question.

Any persons accustomed to visit among the poor in a large district, would, I believe, when confining themselves to a much smaller one, be led, if not to very unexpected conclusions, at least to very curious problems. In dealing with a large number of cases the urgency is so great, one passes over the most difficult questions to work where sight is clear; and one is apt to forget Sissy Jupe's quick sympathetic perception that percentage signifies literally nothing to the friends of the special sufferer, who surely is not worth less than a sparrow. The individual case, if we cared enough for it, would often give us the key to many.

Whoever will limit his gaze to a few persons, and try to solve the problems of their lives—planning, for instance, definitely, how he, even with superior advantages of education, self-control, and knowledge, could bring up a given family on given wages, allowing the smallest amount conceivably sufficient for food, rent, clothes, fuel, and the rest—he may find it in most cases a much more difficult thing than he had ever thought, and sometimes may be an impossibility. It may lead to strange self-questioning about wages. Again, if people will watch carefully the different effect of self-help and of alms, how the latter, like the outdoor relief system under the old Poor-Law, tends to lower wages, undermines the providence of the poor, it may make them put some searching questions to themselves upon the wisdom of backing up wages with gifts. Then they may begin to consider practically whether in their own small sphere they can form no schemes of help, which shall be life-giving, stimulating hope, energy, foresight, self-denial, and choice of right rather than wrong expenditure.

They may earnestly strive to discover plans of help which shall free them from the oppressive responsibility of deciding whether aid is deserved—a question often complicated inextricably with another, namely, whether at a given moment there is a probability of reformation. All of us have felt the impossibility of deciding either question fairly, yet we have been convinced that gifts coming at the wrong time are often deadly. Earnest workers feel a heavy weight on their hearts and consciences from the conviction that the old command "Judge not" is a divine one, and yet that the distribution of alms irrespective of character is fatal. These difficulties lead to variable action, which is particularly disastrous with the poor. But there are plans which cultivate the qualities wherein they are habitually wanting, namely, self-control, energy, prudence, and industry; and such plans, if we will do our part, may be ready at any moment for even the least deserving, and for those who have fallen lowest.

Further details as to modes of help must vary infinitely with circumstances and character. But I may mention a few laws which become clearer and clearer to me as I work.

It is best strictly to enforce fulfillment of all such duties as payment of rent, etc.

It is far better to give work than either money or goods.

It is most helpful of all to strengthen by sympathy and counsel the energetic effort which shall bear fruit in time to come.

It is essential to remember that each man has his own view of his life, and must be free to fulfill it; that in many ways he is a far better judge of it than we, as he has lived through and felt what we have only seen. Our work is rather to bring him to the point of considering, and to the spirit of judging rightly, than to consider or judge for him.

The poor of London (as of all large towns) need the development of every power which can open to them noble sources of joy.

1. The ultimate step taken to enforce payment of rent is to send in a broker to distrain.

BLANK COURT; OR, LANDLORDS AND TENANTS.

October, 1871.

THREE ladies were standing, not long ago, in a poor and dingy court in London, when a group of dirty-faced urchins exclaimed, in a tone, partly of impudence and partly of fun: "What a lot o' landladies, this morning!"

The words set me thinking, for I felt that the boys' mirth was excited, not only by the number of landladies (or of ladies acting as such), but also, probably, by the contrast between these ladies and the landladies they usually saw. For the landlady to the London poor is too often a struggling, cheated, much-worried, long-suffering woman; soured by constant dealing with untrustworthy people; embittered by loss; a prey to the worst lodgers, whom she allows to fall into debt, and is afraid to turn out, lest she should lose the amount they owe her; without spirit or education to enable her to devise improvements, or capital to execute them—never able, in short, to use the power given her by her position to bring order into the lives of her tenants: being, indeed, too frequently entirely under their control. There is a numerous class of landladies worse even than this—bullying, violent, passionate, revengeful, and cowardly. They alternately cajole and threaten, but rarely intend to carry out either their promises or their threats. Severe without principle, weakly indulgent towards evil, given to lying and swearing, too covetous to be drunken, yet indulgent to any lodger who will "treat" them; their influence is incalculably mischievous.

Ought this to be the idea suggested by the word "landlady" to the poor of our cities? The old word "landlord" is a proud one to many an English gentleman, who holds dominion over the neat cottage, with its well-stocked garden; over the comfortable farm-house; over broad, sloping parks, and rich farm-lands. It is a delight to him to keep thus fair the part of the earth over which it has been given him to rule. And, as to his people, he would think it shameful to receive the rents from his well-managed estates in the country, year by year, without some slight recognition of his tenantry—at least on birthdays or at Christmas.

But where are the owners, or lords, or ladies, of most courts like that in which I stood with my two fellow-workers? Who holds dominion there? Who heads the tenants there? If any among the nobly born, or better educated, own them, do they bear the mark of their hands? And if they do *not* own them, might they not do so? There are in those courts as loyal English hearts as ever loved or reverenced the squire in the village, only they have been so forgotten. Dark under the level ground, in kitchens damp with foulest moisture, there they huddle in multitudes, and no one loves or raises them. It must not be thought that the over-worked clergymen and missionaries, heroic as they often are, can do all that might be done for them. They count their flock by thousands, and these people want watching one by one. The clergy have no control over these places, nor have they half the power of directing labor to useful ends, which those might have who owned the houses, and were constantly brought into direct contact with the people.

How this relation of landlord and tenant might be established in some of the lowest districts of London, and with what results, I am about to describe by relating what has been done in the last two years in Blank Court. I have already, in these pages,[1] given an account of my former efforts to establish this relation on a healthy footing in another London court; of the details of my plan of action; and of its success. I am not, therefore, in what follows, putting forth anything new in its main idea, but am simply insisting on principles of the truth of which every day's experience only makes me the more deeply assured, and recounting the history of an attempt to spread those principles to a class still lower than that alluded to in my former paper.

It was near the end of 1869 that I first heard that a good many houses in Blank Court were to be disposed of. Eventually, in the course of that year, six ten-roomed houses were bought by the Countess of Ducie, and five more by another lady, and placed partially under my care. I was especially glad to obtain some influence here, as I knew this place to be one of the worst in Marylebone; its inhabitants were mainly costermongers and small hawkers, and were almost the poorest class of those amongst our population who have any settled home, the next grade below them being vagrants who sleep in common lodging-houses; and I knew that its moral standing was equally low. Its reputation had long been familiar to me; for when unruly and hopeless tenants were sent away from other houses in the district, I had often heard that they had gone to Blank Court, the tone in which it was said implying that they had now sunk to the lowest depths of degradation. A lawyer friend had also said to me, on hearing that it was proposed to buy houses there, "Blank Court! why, that is the place one is always noticing in the police reports for its rows."

Yet its outward appearance would not have led a casual observer to guess its real character. Blank Court is not far from Cavendish Square, and daily in the season, scores of carriages, with their gayly dressed occupants, pass the end of it. Should such look down it, they would little divine its inner life. Seen from the outside, and in the daytime, it is a quiet-looking place, the houses a moderate size, and the space between them tolerably wide. It has no roadway, but is nicely enough paved, and old furniture stands out for sale on the pavement, in front of the few shops.

But if any one had entered those houses with me two years ago, he would have seen enough to surprise and horrify him. In many of the houses the dustbins were utterly unapproachable, and cabbage-leaves, stale fish, and every sort of dirt were lying in the passages and on the stairs; in some the back kitchen had been used as a dustbin, but had not been emptied for years, and the dust filtered through into the front kitchens, which were the sole living and sleeping rooms of some families; in some, the kitchen stairs were many inches thick with dirt, which was so hardened that a shovel had to be used to get it off; in some there was hardly any water to be had; the wood was eaten away, and broken away; windows were smashed; and the rain was coming through the roofs. At night it was still worse; and during the first winter I had to collect the rents chiefly then, as the inhabitants, being principally costermongers, were out nearly all day, and they were afraid to entrust their rent to their neighbors. It was then that I saw the houses in their most dreadful aspect. I well remember wet, foggy, Monday nights, when I turned down the dingy court, past the brilliantly-lighted public-house at the corner, past the old furniture outside the shops, and dived into the dark, yawning, passage ways. The front doors stood open day and night, and as I felt my way down the kitchen stairs, broken, and rounded by the hardened mud upon them, the foul smells which the heavy, foggy air would not allow to rise, met me as I descended, and the plaster rattled down with a hollow sound as I groped along. It was truly appalling to think that there were human beings who lived habitually in such an atmosphere, with such surroundings. Sometimes I had to open the kitchen door myself, after knocking several times in vain, when a woman, quite drunk, would be lying on the floor on some black mass which served as a bed; sometimes, in answer to my knocks, a half-drunken man would swear, and thrust the rent-money out to me through a chink of the door, placing his foot against it, so as to prevent it from opening wide enough to admit me. Always it would be shut again without a light being offered to guide me up the pitch-dark stairs. Such was Blank Court in the winter of 1869. Truly, a wild, lawless, desolate little kingdom to come to rule over.

On what principles was I to rule these people? On the same that I had already tried, and tried with success, in other places, and which I may sum up as the two following:

firstly, to demand a strict fulfillment of their duties to me,—one of the chief of which would be the punctual payment of rent; and secondly, to endeavor to be so unfailingly just and patient, that they should learn to trust the rule that was over them.

With regard to details, I would make a few improvements at once—such, for example, as the laying on of water and repairing of dustbins, but, for the most part, improvements should be made only by degrees, as the people became more capable of valuing and not abusing them. I would have the rooms distempered, and thoroughly cleansed, as they became vacant, and then they should be offered to the more cleanly of the tenants. I would have such repairs as were not immediately needed, used as a means of giving work to the men in times of distress. I would draft the occupants of the underground kitchens into the upstair rooms, and would ultimately convert the kitchens into bath-rooms and wash-houses. I would have the landlady's portion of the house—*i. e.* the stairs and passages—at once repaired and distempered, and they should be regularly scrubbed, and, as far as possible, made models of cleanliness, for I knew, from former experience, that the example of this would, in time, silently spread itself to the rooms themselves, and that payment for this work would give me some hold over the elder girls. I would collect savings personally, not trust to their being taken to distant banks or saving clubs. And finally, I knew that I should learn to feel these people as my friends, and so should instinctively feel the same respect for their privacy and their independence, and should treat them with the same couresy that I should show towards any other personal friends. There would be no interference, no entering their rooms uninvited, no offer of money or the necessaries of life. But when occasion presented itself, I should give them any help I could, such as I might offer without insult to other friends—sympathy in their distresses; advice, help, and counsel in their difficulties; introductions that might be of use to them; means of education; visits to the country; a lent book when not able to work; a bunch of flowers brought on purpose; an invitation to any entertainment, in a room built at the back of my own house, which would be likely to give them pleasure. I am convinced that one of the evils of much that is done for the poor springs from the want of delicacy felt, and courtesy shown, towards them, and that we cannot beneficially help them in any spirit different to that, in which we help those who are better off. The help may differ in amount, because their needs are greater. It should not differ in kind.

To sum up: my endeavors in ruling these people should be to maintain perfect strictness in our business relations, perfect respectfulness in our personal relations.

These principles of government and plans of action were not theoretical: they had not been *thought out* in the study, but had been *worked out* in the course of practical dealings with individual cases. And though I am able thus to formulate them, I want it understood that they are essentially living, that they are not mere dead rules, but principles the application of which is varying from day to day. I can say, for example, "It is our plan to keep some repairs as employment for men out of work;" but it needs the true instinct to apply this plan beneficially—the time to give the work, its kind, its amount, above all the mode of offering it, have to be felt out fresh on each fresh occasion, and the circumstances and characters vary so that each case is new.

The practical carrying out in Blank Court of these various plans of action involved, as may readily be imagined, a great deal of personal supervision. Hence the "lot o'landladies" which excited the attention of the street boys. Several ladies, whether owners of houses or not, have worked there energetically with me since the property was bought; and when I use the word "we," I would have it understood to apply to these ladies and myself: it is often upon them that much of the detail of the work devolves.

But to proceed with the history of Blank Court. Our first step on obtaining possession was to call on all the inhabitants to establish our claim to receive rents. We accepted or refused the people as tenants, made their acquaintance, and learnt all they might be disposed to tell us about themselves and their families. We came upon strange scenes sometimes. In one room a handsome, black, tangle-haired, ragged boy and girl, of about nine and ten, with wild dark eyes, were always to be found, sometimes squatting near the fire, watching a great black pot, sometimes amusing themselves with cutting paper into strips with scissors. It was difficult to extract a word: the money and dirty rent-book were generally pushed to us in silence. No grown person was ever to be seen. For months I never saw these children in the open air. Often they would lie in bed all day long; and I believe they were too ignorant and indolent to care to leave the house except at night, when the boy, as we afterwards found, would creep like a cat along the roofs of the outbuildings to steal lumps of coal from a neighboring shed.

At one room we had to call again and again, always finding the door locked. At last, after weeks of vain effort, I found the woman who owned the room at home. She was sitting on the floor at tea with another woman, the tea being served on an inverted hamper. I sat down on an opposite hamper, which was the only other piece of furniture in the room, and told her I was sorry that I had never been able to make her acquaintance before. To which she replied, with rather a grand air and a merry twinkle in her eye, that she had been "unavoidably absent:" in other words, some weeks in prison,—not a rare occurrence for her.

When we set about our repairs and alterations, there was much that was discouraging. The better class of people in the court were hopeless of any permanent improvement. When one of the tenants of the shops saw that we were sending workmen into the empty rooms, he said considerately, "I'll tell you what it is, Miss, it'll cost you a lot o' money to repair them places, and it's no good. The women's 'eads 'll be druv through the door panels again in no time, and the place is good enough for such cattle as them there." But we were not to be deterred.

On the other hand, we were not to be hurried in our action by threats. These were not wanting. For no sooner did the tenants see the workmen about than they seemed to think that if they only clamored enough they would get their own rooms put to rights. Nothing had been done for years. Now, they thought, was their opportunity. More than one woman locked me in her room with her, the better to rave and storm. She would shake the rent in her pocket to tempt me with the sound of the money, and roar out "that never a farthing of it would she pay till her grate was set," or her floor was mended, as the case might be. Perfect silence would make her voice drop lower and lower, until at last she would stop, wondering that no violent answers were hurled back at her, and a pause would ensue. I felt that promises would be little believed in, and, besides, I wished to feel free to do as much, and only as much, as seemed best to me; so that my plan was to trust to my deeds to speak for themselves, and inspire confidence as time went on. In such a pause, therefore, I once said to a handsome, gypsy-like Irishwoman, "How long have you lived here?" "More than four years," she replied, her voice swelling again at the remembrance of her wrongs; "and always was a good tenant, and paid my way, and never a thing done! And my grate, etc., etc., etc." "And how long have I had the houses?" "Well, I suppose since Monday week," in a gruff but somewhat mollified tone. "Very well, Mrs. L——, just think over quietly what has been done in the houses since then; and if you like to leave and think you can suit yourself better, I am glad you should make yourself comfortable. Meantime, of course, while you stay, you pay rent. I will call for it this evening if it doesn't suit you to pay now. Good morning."

Almost immediately after the purchase of the houses, we had the accumulated refuse of years carted away, the pavement in the yards and front areas were repaired, dustbins cleared, the drains put in order, and water supplied. Such improvements as these are tolerably unspoilable, but for any of a more destructible nature it was better to wait. The importance of advancing slowly, and of gaining some hold over the people as a necessary accompaniment to any real improvement in their dwellings, was perpetually apparent. Their habits were so degraded that we had to work a change in these before they would make any proper use of the improved surroundings we were prepared to give them. We had locks torn off, windows broken, drains stopped, dustbins misused in every possible manner, even pipes broken, and water-taps wrenched away. This was sometimes the result of carelessness, and deeply-rooted habit of dirt and untidiness; sometimes the damage was willful. Our remedy was to watch the right moment for furnishing these appliances, to persevere in supplying them, and to get the people by degrees to work with us for their preservation. I have learned to know that people are ashamed to abuse a place they find cared for. They will add dirt to dirt till a place is pestilential, but the more they find done for it, the more they will respect it, till at last order and cleanliness prevail. It is this feeling of theirs, coupled with the fact that they do not like those whom they have learned to love, and whose standard is higher than their own, to see things which would grieve them, which has enabled us to accomphsh nearly every reform of outward things that we have achieved; so that the surest way to have any place kept clean is to go through it often yourself. First I go at regular times, and then they clean to receive me, and have the pleasure of preparing for me, and seeing my satisfaction; then I go at unexpected times to raise them to the power of having it always clean.

Our plan of removing the inhabitants of the miserable underground kitchens to rooms in the upper parts of the houses, did not, strange as it may seem, meet with any approbation at first. They had been so long in the semi-darkness that they felt it an effort to move. One woman, in particular, I remember, pleaded hard with me to let her stop, saying, "My bits of things won't look *anything* if you bring them to the light." By degrees, however, we effected the change.

I mentioned in my summary of our plan of operations, our custom of using some of the necessary, yet not immediately wanted repairs, as a means of affording work to the tenants in slack times. I lay great stress upon this. Though the men are not mechanics, there are many rough jobs of plastering, distempering, glazing, or sweeping away and removing rubbish which they can do. When, therefore, a tenant is out of work, instead of reducing his energy by any gifts of money, we simply, whenever the funds at our disposal allow it, employ him in restoring and purifying the houses. And what a difference five shillings worth of work in a bad week will make to a family! The father, instead of idling listlessly at the corner of the street, sets busily and happily to work, prepares the whitewash, mends the plaster, distempers the room; the wife bethinks herself of having a turn-out of musty corners or drawers, untouched, maybe, for months, of cleaning her windows, perhaps even of putting up a clean blind; and thus a sense of decency, the hope of beginning afresh and doing better, comes like new life into the home.

The same cheering and encouraging sort of influence, though in a less degree, is exercised by our plan of having a little band of scrubbers. We have each passage scrubbed twice a week by one of the elder girls. The sixpence thus earned is a stimulus, and they often take an extreme interest in the work itself. One little girl was so proud of her first cleaning that she stood two hours watching her passage lest the boys, whom she considered as the natural enemies of order and cleanliness, should spoil it before I came to see it. And one woman remarked to her neighbor how nice the stairs looked. "They haven't been cleaned," she added, "since ever I came into this house." She had been there six years! The effect of these clean passages frequently spreads to the rooms, as the dark line of demarkation between the cleaned passage and the still dirty room arouses the attention, and begins to trouble the minds, of its inmates.

Gradually, then, these various modes of dealing with our little realm began to tell. Gradually the people began to trust us; and gradually the houses were improved. The sense of quiet power and sympathy soon made itself felt, and less and less was there any sign of rudeness or violence towards ourselves. Even before the first winter was over many a one would hurry to light us up the stairs, and instead of my having the rent-book and money thrust to me through the half-open door, and being kept from possible entrance by a firmly planted foot, my reception would be, "Oh, can't you come in, Miss, and sit down for a bit?" Little by little the houses were renovated, the grates reset, the holes in the floors repaired, the cracking, dirty plaster replaced by a clean smooth surface, the heaps of rubbish removed, and we progressed towards order.

Amongst the many benefits which the possession of the houses enables us to confer on the people, perhaps one of the most important is our power of saving them from neighbors who would render their lives miserable. It is a most merciful thing to protect the poor from the pain of living in the next room to drunken, disorderly people. "I am dying," said an old woman to me the other day: "I wish you would put me where I can't hear S—— beating his wife. Her screams are awful. And B——, too, he do come in so drunk. Let me go over the way to No. 30." Our success depends on duly arranging the inmates: not too many children in any one house, so as to overcrowd it; not too few, so as to overcrowd another; not two bad people side by side, or they drink together; not a terribly bad person beside a very respectable one.

Occasionally we come upon people whose lives are so good and sincere, it is only by such services and the sense of our friendship, that we can help them at all; in all important things they do not need our teaching, while we may learn much from them. In one of the underground kitchens, I found an old woman who had been living there for twelve years. In spite of every obstacle, and in the midst of such surroundings as I have described, she was spotlessly clean and had done the very best for the wretched place: the broken bars of the grate she had bound in their places with little bits of wire; the great rents in the wall, one of which went right through to the open air, she had stuffed with rags, the jagged ends of which she had actually taken the trouble to trim neatly with scissors;

she had papered the walls, and as they were so damp that the paste was perpetually losing its hold, she patiently fastened up the long strips of paper fresh every week. With all this work for it she had naturally become so fond of her little home that it nearly broke her heart to think of leaving it. So we determined not to tear her away from it. After a time, however, the force of our former arguments told upon her, and suddenly, one day, she volunteered to move. She has kept her new room, as one would expect, in a state of neatness and order that is quite perfect. She has since been growing less and less able to work, but she has always paid her rent, she has never asked for help, nor would she even accept the small boon of my lending her some money until she could give the due notice which would enable her to draw out her own savings from the bank where she had placed them. She has lived thirty-five years in London, a single woman depending entirely on herself, without parish allowance or other aid, and has had strength to keep up her standard of cleanliness and independence, and a spirit of patient trustfulness that is unfailing. Her life on earth is nearly over; she is now confined to her bed, for the most part quite alone, without even a bell to summon aid: yet there she lies in her snow-white bed as quietly as a little child settling itself to sleep, talking sometimes with a little pride of her long life's work, sometimes with tenderness of her old days in Ireland long ago, and saying gently that she does not wish to be better; she wants to go "home." Even in the extremity of her loneliness only a small mind could pity her. It is a life to watch with reverence and admiration.

We can rarely speak of the depths of the hearts we learn to know or the lives we see in the course of our work. The people are our friends. But sometimes, when such as this old woman seem to have passed beyond us all and to have entered into a quiet we cannot break, we may just glance at a life which, in its simplicity and faithfulness, might make the best of us ashamed.

Since we began our work in the court there has been a marked improvement in many of the people. I may just say, as examples, that the passionate Irish tenant who locked me into her room did not leave us, but has settled down happily, and has shown me more than one act of confidence and kindly feeling; that the old woman whose "bits o' things" would look nothing if brought upstairs, after having been long in a light room, has now asked for a larger one, having freed herself from a debt which cramped her resources, and has begun to save; and that the two dark-eyed children were ultimately won over to trust in us. Their mother—a most degraded woman—when she at last appeared, proved to be living a very disreputable life, and the only hope for the children was to get them away from her influence. My first triumph was in getting the girl to exert herself enough to become one of our scrubbers, and finally, a year ago, we were able to persuade her to go to a little industrial school in the country, where she has since been joined by a sister of hers, who turned up subsequently to my first visits. Unfortunately the mother absconded, taking the boy with her, while we were still hoping to get him sent away to a training-school also; but, even in the short time that he remained with us, I had got some hold over him. By dint of making an agreement with him that I would myself fetch him at eight one morning, and help him to prepare his toilet so as to be fit for the nearest ragged school, I got him to begin learning; and when once the ice was broken, he went frequently of his own accord.

Opportunities for helping people at some important crisis of their lives not unfrequently present themselves. For instance, soon after we came into possession of Blank Court, I once or twice received rent from a young girl, whom I generally found sitting sadly in a nearly bare room, holding in her arms a little baby. She looked so young that I thought at first the baby must be her sister, but it turned out to be her own child. Her husband seemed a mere boy, and was, in fact, only nineteen. One day, when the rent was not forthcoming, I learnt their story. It appeared that an aunt had promised the lad a sovereign to set him up as a costermonger, if he married the girl; but he had not bargained for prepayment, and the promise was not fulfilled. This marriage-portion, which was to have procured them a stock of herrings, had never been forthcoming. This seemed an occasion upon which a small loan might be of the utmost use. I accordingly lent them the much-needed sovereign (which they have since punctually repaid), and thus saved the young couple from being driven to the workhouse, and gave them a small start in life.

To show further the various opportunities afforded us by our footing with the people, I will describe one of our weekly collections of savings.

On Saturday evenings, about eight o'clock, the tenants know that we are to be found in the "club room" (one of the former shops of the court, and now used by us for a men's club, and for boys' and girls' evening classes, as well as for this purpose of collecting savings), and that they may come to us there if they like, either for business or a friendly chat.

Picture a low, rather long room, one of my assistants and myself sitting in state, with pen and ink and bags for money, at a deal table under a flaring gas jet; the door, which leads straight into the court, standing wide open. A bright red blind, drawn down over the broad window, prevents the passers-by from gazing in there, but, round the open door, there are gathered a set of wild, dirty faces looking in upon us. Such a semicircle they make, as the strong gas-light falls upon them! They are mostly children with disheveled hair, and ragged, uncared-for clothes; but, above them, now and then one sees the haggard face of a woman hurrying to make her Saturday evening purchases, or the vacant stare of some half-drunken man. The grown-up people who stop to look in are usually strangers, for those who know us generally come in to us. "Well! they've give it this time, anyhow," one woman will exclaim, sitting down on a bench near us, so engrossed in the question of whether she obtains a parish allowance that she thinks "they" can mean no one but the Board of Guardians, and "it" nothing but the much-desired allowance. "Yes, I thought I'd come in and tell you," she will go on; "I went up Tuesday—" And then will follow the whole story.

"Well, and how do you find yourself, Miss?" a big Irish laborer in a flannel jacket will say, entering afterwards; "I just come in to say I shall be knocked off Monday; finished our job across the park: and if so be there's any little thing in whitewashing to do, why, I'll be glad to do it."

"Presently," we reply, nodding to a thin, slight woman at the door. She has not spoken, but we know the meaning of that beseeching look. She wants us to go up and get her husband's rent from him before he goes out to spend more of it in drink.

The eager, watchful eyes of one of our little scrubbers next attract attention; there she stands, with her savings' card in her hand, waiting till we enter the sixpence she has earned from us during the week. "How much have I got?" she says, eying the written sixpences with delight, "because mother says, please, I'm to draw out next Saturday; she's going to buy me a pair of boots."

"Take two shillings on the card and four shillings rent," a proudly happy woman will say, as she lays down a piece of bright gold, a rare sight this in the court, but her husband has been in regular work for some little time.

"Please, Miss," says another woman, "will you see and do something for Jane? She's that masterful since her father died, I can't do nothing with her, and she'll do no good in this court. Do see and get her a place somewheres away."

A man will enter now: "I'll leave you my rent to-night, Miss, instead o' Monday, please; it'll be safer with you than with me."

A pale woman comes next, in great sorrow. Her husband, she tells us, has been arrested without cause. We believe this to be true; the man has always paid his way honestly, worked industriously, and lived decently. So my assistant goes round to the police-station at once to bail him, while I remain to collect the savings. "Did he seem grateful?" I say to her on her return. "He took it very quietly," is her answer; "he seemed to feel it quite natural that we should help him."

Such are some of the scenes on our Savings' evenings; such some of the services we are called upon to render; such the kind of footing we are on with our tenants. An evening such as this assuredly shows that our footing has somewhat changed since those spent in Blank Court during the first winter.

My readers will not imagine that I mean to imply that there are not still depths of evil remaining in Blank Court. It would be impossible for such a place as I described it as being originally, to be raised in two years to a satisfactory condition. But, what I do contend is, that we have worked some very real reforms, and seen some very real results. I feel that it is in a very great degree a question of time, and that, now that we have got hold of the hearts of the people, the court is sure to improve steadily. It will pay as good a percentage to its owners and will benefit its tenants as much as any of the other properties under my management have done. This court contains two out of eight properties on which the same plans have been tried, and all of them are increasingly prosperous. The first two were purchased by Mr. Ruskin.

It appears to me then to be proved by practical experience, that when we can induce the rich to undertake the duties of landlord in poor neighborhoods, and insure a sufficient amount of the wise, personal supervision of educated and sympathetic people acting as their representatives, we achieve results which are not attainable in any other way. It is true that there are Dwellings' Improvement Societies, and the good these societies do is incalculable; I should be the last to underrate it. But it is almost impossible that any society could do much for such places as Blank Court, because it is there not so much a question of dealing with houses alone, as of dealing with houses in connection with their influence on the character and habits of the people who inhabit them. If any society had come there and put those houses into a state of perfect repair at once, it would have been of little use, because its work would have been undone again by the bad habits and carelessness of the people. If improvements were made on a large scale, and the people remained untouched, all would soon return to its former condition. You cannot deal with the people and their houses separately. The principle on which the whole work rests, is that the inhabitants and their surroundings must be improved together. It has never yet failed to succeed.

Finally, I would call upon those who may possess cottage property in large towns, to consider the immense power they thus hold in their hands, and the large influence for good they may exercise by the wise use of that power. When they have to delegate it to others, let them take care to whom they commit it; and let them beware lest, through the widely prevailing system of sub-letting, this power ultimately abide with those who have neither the will nor the knowledge which would enable them to use it beneficially;—with such as the London landladies described at the beginning of this paper. The management of details will seldom remain with the large owners, but they may choose trustworthy representatives, and retain at least as much control over their tenants, and as much interest in them, as is done by good landlords in the country.

And I would ask those who do *not* hold such property to consider whether they might not, by possessing themselves of some, confer lasting benefits on their poorer neighbors?

In these pages I have dwelt mainly on the way our management affects the people, as I have given elsewhere[2] my experiences as to financial matters and details of practical management. But I may here urge one thing on those about to undertake to deal with such property, the extreme importance of enforcing the punctual payment of rents. This principle is a vital one. Firstly, because it strikes one blow at the credit system, that curse of the poor; secondly, because it prevents large losses from bad debts, and prevents the tenant from believing that he will be suffered to remain, whatever his conduct may be, resting that belief on his knowledge of the large sum that would be lost were he turned out; and, thirdly, because the mere fact that the man is kept up to his duty is a help to him, and increases his self-respect and hope of doing better.

I would also say to those who, in the carrying out of such an undertaking, are brought into immediate contact with the tenants, that its success will depend most of all on their giving sympathy to the tenants, and awakening confidence in them; but it will depend also in a great degree on their power of bestowing concentrated attention on small details.

For the work is one of detail. Looking back over the years as they pass, one sees a progress that is *not* small; but day after day the work is one of such small things, that if one did not look beyond and through them they would be trying. Locks to be mended, notices to be served, the missing shilling of the week's rent to be called for three or four times, petty quarrels to be settled, small rebukes to be spoken, the same remonstrances to be made again and again.

But it is on these things and their faithful execution that the life of the whole matter depends, and by which steady progress is insured. It is the small things of the world that color the lives of those around us, and it is on persistent efforts to reform these that progress depends; and we may rest assured that they who see with greater eyes than ours have a due estimate of the service, and that if we did but perceive the mighty principles underlying these tiny things we should rather feel awed that we are entrusted with them at all, than scornful and impatient that they are no larger. What are we that we should ask for more than that God should let us work for Him among the tangible things which He created to be fair, and the human spirits which He redeemed to be pure? From time to time He lifts a veil and shows us, even while we struggle with imperfections here below, that towards which we are working—shows us how, by governing and ordering the tangible things one by one, we may make of this earth a fair dwelling-place. And far better still, how by cherishing human beings He will let us help Him in His work of building up temples meet for Him to dwell in—faint images of that best temple of all, which

He promised that He would raise up on the third day, though men might destroy it.

OCTAVIA HILL.

-

1. *Macmillan's Magazine* for July, 1869.
2. Cottage Property in London.—*Fortnightly Review,* Nov. 1, 1866.
    Organized Work amongst the Poor.—*Macmillan's Magazine,* July, 1869.

THE WORK OF VOLUNTEERS IN THE ORGANIZATION OF CHARITY.

IT is clear to those who are watching the work closely, and must even be apparent to those less conversant with the subject, that a great and growing conviction is abroad that our charitable efforts need concentrating, systematizing, and uniting. There are many signs that this conviction is bearing practical fruit. All the thirty Poor-Law districts into which London is divided are now provided with committees for organizing charitable relief. The formation of these committees has led gentlemen specially interested in the subject to come forward in various parts of London as candidates for the office of guardians; several such candidates have been elected in St. George's, Kensington, Marylebone, and other parishes. Nor is the movement confined to London. Charity Organization Societies, or others of a kindred nature, have been established in most of the large towns of England and Scotland. Conversation, newspapers, conferences, all bear witness how very generally it is now recognized that something ought to be done to improve our system of charitable relief, some co-operation secured between Poor-Law and charity, and some efficient means adopted to render alms less pauperizing than they have hitherto been. It is becoming clear to the public that there is a right and a wrong, a wise and an unwise charity. Those who have the interests of the poor at heart are learning, more and more, to consult experienced people before taking any direct steps towards trying to help those who apply to them for aid; those who wish to give money beginning to entrust it to enlightened committees, instead of endeavoring to distribute it themselves.

It becomes almost needless now to charge on the evils of "overlapping,"—that is, of various charitable agencies covering the same ground whilst ignorant of each other's proceedings; or to dwell on the cruelty of the utter want of system which has hitherto prevailed,—to point to poor families assisted by three or four agencies at times when they needed help least, and others neglected by all at times when they needed it most. It would not be difficult to give examples of these evils, and to show that they are inseparable from the condition of large towns wherever nothing is done to secure unity of action amongst those who are trying to assist the poor.

Much has been done. The evils of overlapping, on the one hand, and of neglect on the other, are being swept away wherever organization committees, with their machinery for thorough investigation, and relief societies, with their power to assist, are in existence. By means of this system of inquiry into the merits of cases a great degree of uniformity in dealing with them is secured; no relief is given without due consideration, no poor person who chooses to apply can fail to have a hearing for his case, and similar needs will meet with a similar response. All this is no small gain. But now a new danger seems to me to be arising; a danger lest, rushing from one extreme to another, we should leave to committees, with their systems of rules, the whole work of charity, and deprive this great organizing movement of all aid from what I may call the personal element. The value of this element seems to me to be inestimable. Charity owes all its graciousness to the sense of its coming from a real friend. We want to bring the rich and poor, the educated and uneducated, more and more into direct communication. We want to enlist the thought, knowledge, sympathy, foresight, and gentleness of the educated in the service of the poor, and must beware of raising up barriers of committees between those who should meet face to face. There is beyond all doubt in almost every town a great amount of volunteer work to be had, which, were it organized and concentrated, would achieve infinitely more than its best efforts can now accomplish. There is always, however, a difficulty in calculating to any great extent on volunteer work, inasmuch as it is apt to be disconnected, desultory, and untrained.

It is true that where an energetic body of visitors is gathered together under able and vigilant guidance— where their districts are small, their visits frequent, their written records simple and complete, and gaps in their ranks quickly filled up, so that their work is not intermittent—they form a powerful agency for good. Such societies are usually the first to see the importance of putting themselves into communication with other charitable bodies; and when they do this, little improvement in the machinery is requisite. But it is also sadly true that the work of a number of earnest and devoted volunteers is thrown away because their districts are too large, their duties indefinite, and their work unconnected with that of others laboring according to any definite plan.

Several things, then, appear to me to be evident—(1), that if the poor are to be raised to a permanently better condition, they must be dealt with as individuals and by individuals; (2), that for this hundreds of workers are necessary; and (3), that this multitude of helpers is to be found amongst volunteers—whose aid, as we arrange things at present, is to a great extent lost. The problem to be solved, therefore, is how to collect our volunteers into a harmonious whole—the action of each being free, yet systematized; and how thus to administer relief through the united agency of corporate bodies and private individuals; how, in fact, to secure all the personal intercourse and friendliness, all the real sympathy, all the graciousness of individual effort, without losing the advantage of having relief voted by a central committee, and according to definite principles. The way in which this problem has been dealt with in one small district of London will be seen in the following pages. Every district will, no doubt, have to deal with the question in a somewhat different way, which must be determined by its special circumstances; but the subjoined sketch of a plan now in operation is given because it is always easier to see how a scheme will work when it comes before us as an actual fact, with a definite place and history, than when its bare principles only are laid down.

The working of the plan is not yet by any means perfect. There are many flaws still to be remedied, many breaks still to be filled up. It might, perhaps, have been better to delay writing about it till the working was made more complete, had it not been that the plan has been successful so far, and that it promises to be increasingly so. Besides, this seems the time when an account of a practical scheme for using individual work in conjunction with that of committees may be of real value. The need of some such scheme is felt with regard to the Poor Law. The Poor Law authorities have lately called the attention of Boards of Guardians to the success of the Elberfield system, which depends on the careful and systematic inquiries of a large number of volunteer visitors. The Macclesfield Board of Guardians has already invited volunteers to aid it under the name of Assistant Guardians. The same want is felt with regard to charity. On all sides we hear of people willing to give their time if only they could be sure of doing good. They are dissatisfied, they say, with district visiting, which creates so much discontent and poverty, and does so little lasting good; they want to know of some way in which their efforts may fit in with more organized work.

In the district in which the following plan has been tried the poorer inhabitants have for years been accustomed to make their applications for relief daily, between nine and ten o'clock, at a house situated in the center of the parish. The mode of administering relief has been changed, but the house is still used for the reception of applications. The names are taken down, and one of the blank forms used by the Charity Organization Society[1] is filled up with the account given by the applicant of himself and his circumstances. The form will then contain a statement of the names and ages, occupation, and earnings of every member of the applicant's family, his present and his previous address, the parish relief he receives (if any), the name of the club or benefit society to which he belongs (if there be such), the particular help he asks for, and the ground of the application. The form is immediately forwarded to the Charity Organization Society, who thoroughly investigate the information it contains by means of a paid officer. It is returned with its statements either verified or contradicted, and now shows, in addition to what it contained before, the report of the relieving officer, that of the minister of any denomination with which the applicant is connected, and his character as given by his previous landlord and other references. On the day when the application is first made, and the Charity Organization Society apprised of it, a post-card or other message is sent to the visitor of the street or court where the applicant resides. This informs her of the application, and also that she is expected to send in on the ensuing Friday any information regarding the case which she may already have, or may learn from a visit paid during the week. She at the same time gives her advice as to the best way of dealing with the application. The Relief Committee (of the constitution of which we will speak presently) meets every Friday evening. They have before them not only the valuable information of the Charity Organization Society, gathered, sifted, and examined by their paid officer and representative Committee, but also the detailed account of a volunteer, who brings to bear on the case a fresher and more personal sympathy than a paid agent ordinarily possesses, who has much more patience to listen to, and probably more patience to elicit the little facts on which so much may depend. Any one will appreciate the value of this who has had experience of the difficulty of obtaining the evidence of uneducated people, women more especially; they are nervously confused, they cannot understand what are the real points of the case, nor state them clearly; often the most important fact of all comes out apparently quite by accident in the middle of a long sentence after the terror of being questioned has worn off. Thus the reports sent in, even by young or inexperienced visitors, bring forward facts which might never have come to the knowledge of the committee, while the reports of more practiced visitors are of still greater value, and not unfrequently suggest far more efficient ways of helping poor families than could have been otherwise devised.

The applicant himself comes before the committee. He can thus explain his prospects, clear up any apparent discrepancy of statement, talk over any new plan proposed by visitor or committee, and receive, without delay, the answer to his application.

Whatever grant is sanctioned, however, or whatever plan of action is suggested, the visitor is entrusted with the management of it, so that where money is given it reaches those helped through a kind friend; and where some plan is recommended, it is tried under the friendly and watchful eyes of one who, owing to the advantages of education, should be wiser in many ways than the applicant. Her power, at any rate, is of a different kind, and may fill in his deficiencies.

The province of the Charity Organization Society is that of investigation only;[2] while the province of the Relief Committee, before whom all the collected information is placed, and before whom the applicant appears, is that of final decision or relief. It dispenses the funds of the district, receiving money from people of all denominations, and administering help to all denominations without distinction. It is composed of two clergymen, one doctor, one schoolmaster, three tradesmen. In order to secure the attendance of men occupied during the day, this committee meets in the evening. One lady, the referee of the Charity Organization, always attends as a medium of communication between the visitors, committee, and Charity Organization Society. Any visitors can attend who wish, but in general they find it more convenient to report by letter. Unless the referee has much time, one paid worker is needed to carry out the work well. In the district just described the former almoner is employed, who has great knowledge of the people. She attends the committee, and her information is found to be most valuable. It is a great advantage to have some one always on the spot. She receives applications, and at once sends notice of them to the visitors and Charity Organization Society. She communicates to the visitors the decision of the committee, pays them money which is voted for applicants living in their districts, and keeps the accounts. In cases of emergency she visits, but her main object ought always to be to bring the visitors in well to their work.

Such is an outline of the plan adopted as regards its main features. Dry and formal as it may appear in print, I think that any one who reflects will see how the most intimate, loving, friendly way of reaching the poor through the efforts of kind visitors (each of whom visits chiefly amongst those she knows best) has been secured, whilst any danger of confusion has been avoided, and the chance of overlapping has been reduced to a minimum.

A few specimens of the kind of cases which may come before the Parish Committee, and of the mode in which they would be dealt with, are here subjoined.

An old woman enters the room. She gives an anxious, nervous glance at the members of the committee who are sitting round the table. She is asked to take a seat and to answer the questions, which are as kindly put to her as possible. Soon, however, she becomes hopelessly confused, and in her long, rambling tale contradicts herself over and over again. It seems to be impossible to discover any reason for her actions—why she lives in so dear a room, why she persistently hides some facts. But reference is made to a note sent by the lady-visitor to the committee. She, in a quiet, friendly talk has found out all the old woman's tale. The committee are thus able to understand why she clings to the room she has lived in for so long, though the rent is high; why she works to keep a lodger, when she might live as cheaply alone; why she refuses to tell the names of those who help her. All is cleared up; and since her relations seem to be doing their duty, and the parish making the largest allowance which the guardians think it right to give outside the workhouse, a pension of two shillings a week is granted her for three months. The visitor will pay this pension, and in her weekly visit the friendship will grow. She, unconsciously, perhaps, will supervise the home, and at the end of three months, when the old woman will appear again to have her pension renewed, she will be able to tell of a life which has become quieter and happier.

Or perhaps a younger woman applies. She will tell how illness and misfortune have reduced herself and her husband to poverty. He has at length gone into the workhouse infirmary, where, possibly, he may linger on for months or years, and she has come to ask for help for herself. The committee see that the only result of a gift would be to destroy her power of self-help and tempt her to lean on the uncertain aid of others, while if they helped her adequately the tax on their own funds would be large, and she would be kept in idleness and prevented from fitting herself for future work. She pleads for a little temporary employment, but they tell her that as she has no children to need her care, she had better at once take a place as domestic servant. She says she is not strong enough for hard work. They elicit, however, that she is a good needlewoman, and therefore advise her to seek a place as young lady's maid, or wardrobe-keeper in a school. Her reply is, "Thank you, but I'd rather muddle on." The committee is no doubt right: its decision will help her to face her future, and to see that it is best now, while she is not old, to find an occupation by which she can permanently support herself. Yet she cannot see it at present in this light, it comes to her too suddenly. In spite of the gentle considerateness of the members of the committee, it must be hard for her to face her fate, receive as it were the verdict, "No more home," from a company of people she never saw before. The decision must seem stern. But that night a letter will be dispatched to the lady who has charge of the district where she lives, telling her the committee's decision; the visitor will gently talk to her, advise her, perhaps find a situation for her; when she has resolved to take one, the visitor will herself write to the committee asking for a grant for an advertisement, or for clothes.

Others apply to whom the committee recommend a course which seems hard. A little sick child must be sent away into the country. The father of a family must go to a Convalescent Hospital. The large and expensive room must be given up by the old couple whose wages are falling lower and lower. The kitchen, the dampness of which is sapping the children's strength, must be left; the idle son must be made to work. The advice of the committee is generally refused, but they need not despair. They know that in a day or two the visitor will call—she will tell the mother how kind are those who care for sick children, and will gradually persuade her to send her little one out of the hot, close air which is killing it. She will tell the man how much better it would be to get thoroughly strong than to work on in his weak state; she will stir him up by thoughts of the bright grounds which surround the Convalescent Hospital: and soon she will come to the committee for the offered letter. Going day by day she will break down the apathy and carelessness which has allowed a high rent or an unhealthy situation so long to cripple the strength of the family. She will tell of better and cheaper rooms, she will appeal to both love and prudence, and by kind words to-day and by stern refusals to-morrow give help till they so far help themselves as to move. She will go to visit those who are bitterly resenting the decision of the committee not to help so long as the strong son remains idle or children are kept away from school. She will speak gently and simply of the blessedness of duties; she will tell of the kindness which has seen so far that it would make the idle industrious, the careless careful, the ignorant wise. Perhaps she will find and talk to the idler or the truants, and them she will induce to go with some of their playmates to school, him she will stir up to apply for the work of which the committee told him. Thus the visitor in her visits will persuade and rouse the people to the action that the committee saw to be good, but were powerless to enforce.

Then there are those who suffer poverty quietly and shrink from making any appeal. These the visitor finds out and sends to the committee for their advice and help. Spirited and hard-working women, high-class working men whose illness has been so long that the club money has ceased, will thus be brought to the notice of the committee, who will go patiently into each case. The woman will probably be offered some work; and though she has a hard life at home, children to care for, and occasional mangling to do, she will make an effort to accept the offer; some means of cure or some quiet work will be proposed to the sick man, or it may be thought well to grant him a regular sum weekly for a time. In all the cases the knowledge of the committee will be brought to bear on the poverty of the striving family that the visitor has discovered.

The visitor, however, may not always appear to advocate assistance; sometimes she comes to discourage it. People will apply whose tale seems good. A man wants work; a girl wants clothes to go to a place. At first it appears as if they would make good use of help. The visitor's report soon gives another aspect to the case. She will tell how on such a date the man had lost his work through drink, or how the help so often received had been misused; it is clear to the committee now that such a man can only learn by being left to himself, and though he cringingly begs for work, it is refused. The visitor will also tell how the girl has been frequently helped to clothes of which she had made no good use, how situation after situation had been carelessly lost, how weak parents and idle companions had always been ready to back her up in bad ways. The committee are thus able to see that now she must be taught to earn her clothes gradually. So only will she learn her responsibilities and reap the natural reward of labor.

It will be seen from the foregoing illustrations that the endeavor of the committee and of those at work under them is to give help that shall be adequate, and as far as possible, permanently beneficial. They feel themselves bound, even though the applicant be deserving, to refuse aid which could be a mere temporary stop-gap and confer no lasting benefit, and their aim is in every case to rouse the spirit of independence and self-help.

It will also have been observed how very valuable an element in the working of the scheme the visitor forms; that she is not only a channel through which useful information reaches the committee, but is, in almost every instance, their actual agent in carrying out the plans of help adopted. I must, however, say something further as to the importance of the appointment of some lady or gentleman acting as *Referee;* that is, as a center for all the volunteers working as visitors. For if volunteer work is to form a useful part of our scheme of dealing with the people, we must accept those as workers whose work is necessarily intermittent. This must be done in order that we may secure a sufficient number of workers, and not waste, but gather in and use all the overflowing sympathy which is such a blessing to giver and receiver. With our volunteers, home claims must and should come first; and it is precisely those whose claims are deepest, and whose family life is the noblest, who have the most precious influence in the homes of the poor. But if the work is to be valuable, we must find some way to bind together broken scraps of time, and thus give it continuity in spite of changes and breaks. One great means of doing this is to have a living center. This should be secured in the referee.

The referee in the district here described was appointed in the first instance by the District Committee of the Charity Organization Society; she was subsequently asked to attend the Relief Committee, and has since been recognized by the Guardians and the sub-committee of the School Board as the representative of all the visitors throughout the district: the guardians kindly send to her, after their weekly meetings, notes of every decision arrived at as to applications for relief; these are immediately passed on by her to the visitor of the particular court where the applicant resides. The School Board has withdrawn its paid agent and entrusted to her and the staff of visitors working in concert with her the working of the compulsory clauses of the Education Act. She thus acts as a connecting link between all the various agencies at work in the parish.

It is evident that catastrophe would ensue if public bodies such as the guardians or School Board attempted to deal directly with such a crude, changeful, and untrained body as our volunteers necessarily form; but, communicating with them through the referee, they can use their aid and find it valuable.

The existence of a referee is a help to the visitors in various ways. She receives applications from all volunteers, introduces them to the clergy and others who need workers, or enrolls them as visitors under the Charity Organization Society in unvisited courts, if such there be. She has nothing to do with their work, so far as it is denominational, but takes note of it so far as it deals with visible help. She introduces temporary or permanent substitutes when visitors are absent from town, or ill, or unable from any other cause to continue their work; so that the threads of it are never broken. She is able to give, in a much more detailed and personal way than any corporate body could do, information as to sources of relief, societies available for special cases, as to what visitors of other denominations are doing, and what help the Poor Law will give. For example: "Can anything be done about Mrs. H— —?" a new visitor will ask; "her room is fearfully dirty, and she is so infirm now that she cannot keep it clean. She would be better off in the workhouse." "I will communicate with the guardians, and no doubt the relieving officer will visit and report," the referee will answer. Or another volunteer will ask, "Can you tell me exactly what the law is now as to compulsory attendance at school? There are several bad cases of neglect in my court—what should I do about them?" Or another: "No. 7 in —— Street is in a most unhealthy state; can nothing be done?" "Yes, certainly," the referee will say; "if the drains are really, as you think, not trapped, the landlord can be compelled to do it. Write to the Inspector of Nuisances, and ask him to look into it. He is always most attentive to a request of this kind." Sometimes the suggestion will come from the referee. "Would you," she will say to some of the ladies, "make a list of the unvaccinated children in your streets, and tell the mothers how and when most easily to get the neglect remedied? They only want a little spurring up." Such is the work the ladies find, and the kind of help the referee can give.

Another most important means of securing unity of action is afforded by the written records which the committee make it a point that the visitors should keep—and should keep according to one fixed and definite plan. Each court has its own separate district book; each applicant has his separate page, where the detail regarding him and his family can be found at once. The reports of the relieving officer, of the clergyman, and of any references the applicant may have given, are all found in a condensed form on this same page. An entry is made of every kind of material help given, summed up in a money column each month; and the visitor is also expected to record every month the principal events which have happened in the family. One line only is allowed for this. This rule is made because MS. records become useless if they are voluminous; the chief events only are required and must be carefully selected. The book is sent in once a month to the referee.

The privacy of the poor is not infringed by the use of these records, since the books remain exclusively in the hands of the visitor and referee, and it rests with the visitor to report to the committee only that which she deems essential to the right decision of a case. And, moreover, nothing of a private nature—nothing which could imply a breach of confidence—ought ever to be entered in the books at all.

The advantages of thus keeping district books are very great. It is of course not unusual for those who visit amongst the poor to keep written records of one kind or another. But if they are kept in various forms and the information is not tabulated so as to be readily comprehended by fellow-workers, half their value is lost. To be available for general use, it is all-important that the books throughout a parish should be *uniform*, and the information contained in them *complete* and *condensed*. They should be arranged so as to bring to a focus all the information obtained through the Charity Organization Society. Now it too often happens that they contain only notes of such facts as have come under the visitor's personal observation, and are kept by each visitor according to a different plan.

The work itself is an always growing one, as the system does not stop at mere relief, but uses its machinery to carry out every plan of helpfulness that can be devised. The visitors find that the work opens out as they themselves increase in power. Then the question arises how the pressing, useful things, which so urgently need doing, can possibly be got through. "I see more to do in my district the longer I work there," one lady said to the referee, not long ago; "the more I learn, the more the work increases. I see numberless helpful things I could do if only I had time. May I divide my district? I don't know which part of it I can make up my mind to give up; there are people I should grieve to lose sight of in every part of it, yet I cannot manage all that I now see ought to be done." "Do not divide your district," the referee replied; "the Committees, Guardians, School Board, and I myself cannot easily treat with still smaller divisions than that into separate courts or streets. Let me introduce you to one of the younger volunteers whom you may associate with you in the work. She is too young to visit alone, or to judge what is wise in difficult cases, but she will write your monthly reports, will be a friendly messenger to pay pensions, will call to ask if children are at school, and report to the School Board, will collect savings and keep accounts of them, will write about admissions to Convalescent Homes or Industrial Schools, will give notice of classes and entertainments, and register the window plants before our flower shows. In short, she will form a friendly link between you and the people, will save your time, and be herself trained to take the lead hereafter. Mr. R., too, offered help in the evening, if you want him to establish that Co-operative Store, to keep some life in the Working Men's Club, or to collect savings in the court on a Saturday night; and Mrs. S. offers help in money for special cases of want which the committee can hardly take up, or for some of our excursions to the country this summer. In fact, it you will associate other workers with you, instead of still further subdividing the district, it will be much the best."

And so the work grows, and the various help gets more and more woven into one whole.

Much has been written of late on the subject of Sisterhoods and of "Homes," where those who wish to devote themselves to the service of the poor can live together,consecrating their whole life to the work. I must here express my conviction that we want very much more the influence that emanates not from "a Home," but from "homes." One looks with reverence on the devotion of those who, leaving domestic life, are ready to sacrifice all in the cause of the poor, and give up time, health, and strength in the effort to diminish the great mass of sin and sorrow that is in the world. I have seen faces shining like St. Stephen's with sight of heaven beyond the pain and sin. I have seen shoulders bent as St. Christopher's might have been—better in angels' sight than upright ones. I have seen hair turned gray by sorrow shared with others. And before such, one bends with reverence. But I am sure we ought to desire to have as workers, joyful, strong, many-sided natures, and that the poor, tenderly as they may cling to those who, as it were, cast in their lots amongst them, are better for the bright visits of those who are strong, happy, and sympathetic.

"Send me," said one day a poor woman, who did not even know the visitor's name, "the lady with the sweet smile and the bright golden hair."

The work amongst the poor is, in short, better done by those who do less of it, or rather, who gain strength and brightness in other ways. I hope for a return to the old fellowship between rich and poor; to a solemn sense of relationship; to quiet life side by side; to men and women coming out from bright, good, simple homes, to see, teach, and learn from the poor; returning to gather fresh strength from home warmth and love, and seeing in their own homes something of the spirit which should pervade all.

I believe that educated people would come forward if once they saw how they could be really useful, and without neglecting nearer claims. Let us reflect that hundreds of workers are wanted; that if they are to preserve their vigor they must not be over-worked; and that each of us who might help and holds back not only leaves work undone, but injures, to a certain extent, the work of others. Let each of us not attempt too much, but take some one little bit of work, and, doing it simply, thoroughly, and lovingly, wait patiently for the gradual spread of good, and leave to professional workers to deal for the present with the great mass of evil around.

To recapitulate, then, let me say that I think the operations of the Charity Organization Society have been wholly beneficial so far, but that it will have to secure more extended personal influence between rich and poor if it is to be permanently successful. As a society it is doing its work; it is contending for justice and order; it has urged us not to corrupt our fellow-citizens; it has instituted inquiries in support of truth; it has responsible officers; it is an upholder of method, and it will help us to be swift, just, and sure in our gifts. But it can never be a more living educational body than the law is. The society can never be a vital, loving, living force; it can never wake up enthusiasm, nor gently lead wanderers, nor stir by unexpected mercy, nor strengthen by repeated words of guidance. The ground once cleared by it, the work remains for individuals to carry on.

OCTAVIA HILL.

-

1. N.B.—To save confusion, the District Committee of the Charity Organization Society is throughout this paper spoken of as the Charity Organization Society. This seemed the simplest way to distinguish it from the Relief Committee.

2. "The Charity Organization Society" is the short title of "The Society for Organizing Charitable Relief and Repressing Mendicity," which was established in London in 1869. It was formed with the intention of remedying acknowledged abuses in the administration of charitable relief; and also to repress the profitable trade of mendicity, pnrsned by many who had no claim upon the public for support. The society does not confine its operations to these two branches, but aims at improving the condition of the poor, by enabling them to help themselves rather than by giving them alms. It has, accordingly, originated inquiry into the causes of

distress and poverty, and has issued reports upon night refuges, soup-kitchens, crêches or public day nurseries, dispensaries, district visiting, systematic inquiry into the cases of applicants for relief and employment, and kindred subjects.

The affairs of the society are managed by a central council, holding periodical meetings, and which consists of some of the most influential citizens of London. The chairman and Hon. secretary of each district committee are ex-officio members of the council. There are at present thirty-five of these district committees, or branches, covering nearly the whole area of the metropolis, with its population of quite three millions. Each district committee has its permanent office. In some districts there are two such offices, with a small staff of paid officials; but nearly all the work is done by volunteers. The expenses of the central society are covered by special subscriptions. This fund is entirely distinct from the maintenance funds of the different district committees.

The districts are divided into smaller sub-districts or sub-divisions, usually following the existing legal boundaries; and the co-operation of the resident clergy, of all denominations, is always invited, as well as that of all existing charitable relief agencies. The sub-district in which Miss Octavia Hill has done such a remarkable work is that of St. Mary's, Bryanston Square, a portion of the very large parish and Poor Law district of St. Marylebone, London. Co-operation has here been secured between four agencies engaged in the administration of charitable relief. These are the Board of Guardians of the Poor, answering to our City Commissioners of Charities or County Superintendents of the Poor; the St. Marylebone District Committee of the Charity Organization Society; the Relief Committee, and the District Visitors. Miss Hill acts as Referee for all. She is the medium of communication through which each agency knows what the other is doing, thus enabling it to deal intelligently with each case of distress which comes before it. The visitors also obtain information for the School Board.—ED.

RELIEF—OFFICIAL AND VOLUNTEER AGENCIES IN ADMINISTERING.

10th January, 1874.

Sir:

In accordance with your request, I beg to furnish an account of the system now in operation in a part of the parish of Marylebone, which aims at establishing a complete combination of official and volunteer agencies in dealing with Poor Law cases.

The attention of Poor-Law reformers has been much directed of late years to the administration of out-door relief in Elberfeld. The success of the system pursued there is no longer doubtful. It has been in operation for years; and the report presented to the Local Government Board by their inspector, after his visit, has proved how powerful it is in diminishing pauperism. In the first place, it is shown that the employment of numerous volunteer visitors has there formed a check on imposture, such as our relieving officers, owing to the size of their districts, cannot possibly supply; and secondly, that it has been found possible to adopt there much more radical measures for removing poverty than are here adopted. The poor are divided into groups, each group consisting of a few families, and each cluster of families is committed to the special care and supervision of an intelligent visitor, who goes in and out among them, making himself acquainted with their daily lives, their past history, their present resources and circumstances.

This being so, an account of an organization based on the same principles, and existing in our own country, gains an interest which it otherwise would not possess, and claims attention, though it covers a small area only, though it is tentative, and has not as yet been in operation more than one year. If the scheme succeeds and spreads, we may fairly hope much from it. It is as yet in its infancy, and no formal opinion as to its working has been pronounced by the Marylebone Board of Guardians; but individual members of that Board have expressed their warm approval, the clerk and the relieving officer appear much pleased with the plan, and at present there are no signs of failure, nor does any modification even appear necessary.

I proceed, therefore, to give an account of the system as at present in operation, and will show afterwards its resemblance to the Elberfeld plan, its chief difference from it, and the reason such marked difference is necessary here and now.

At the end of 1872 it came under the notice of the Guardians of St. Marylebone that there existed in a part of their parish—the division known as St. Mary's, Bryanston Square,—a body of district visitors differing in some measure from any to be found in other parts of London. Their special training was due to the fact that soon after the Charity Organization Society was founded, the rector of St. Mary's had determined to reform his system of distributing the funds entrusted to him for charitable purposes, whilst still using the district visitors as his agents. To this end he made over the whole of these funds to a small committee, the St. Mary's Relief Committee, composed of men of various classes, who had given special attention to the wise administration of aid to the poor. Every applicant for help throughout St. Mary's had henceforth to appear before this committee, who were guided in their decision as to his case both by a report from the Marylebone branch of the Charity Organization Society, and by one from the visitor in whose district he resided. Thus a thorough and efficient inquiry was secured. They also aimed at making relief more adequate than formerly; refusing small grants, which would only give temporary and illusory aid, and endeavoring, by means of employment, emigration, loans to enable people to start afresh in life, and so on, to give real and permanent assistance. This committee I was asked to join, as, having a seat on the Marylebone Charity Organization Society, I could form a personal link between the inquiring and the relieving bodies, in addition to the written link which the report on each case afforded. I was also asked to act as referee, that is, to communicate the decisions of the committee to the visitor, who was requested to dispense the aid voted or inform the applicant of the reason of its refusal. In this capacity of referee, I formed a sort of center for the district visitors; it became my duty to give advice when asked, and to instruct new or inexperienced visitors in the nature of their duties and the principles they were expected to adopt. Each visitor had to keep a book, in which the name of every applicant was entered, together with the information obtained about him through the local branch of the Charity Organization Society. An account of all money given to him by any charitable agency, and a short notice from month to month of the events in his family were also entered. Each book contained the facts relating to residents in one court or street only, and was always in the hands of the visitor of that court, temporary or permanent; an alphabetical index enabled her to turn at once to the account of any given family.

The result of this system was to train a body of visitors in judicious and organized modes of work. The light thrown upon cases of applicants by the Charity Organization Society, the advantages afforded by practical work under an experienced committee, and the power of watching individual cases of distress through a long period of their history (a power which small districts and written records materially increase), were all important elements in the education of these visitors.

When this system had been in operation two or three years, it became clear that these volunteer visitors might be valuable to the relieving officer, if they could be brought into communication with him, and that a mass of information had been collected in their district-books, which might be of service to the Guardians if it could be made available at the right moment. But the attempt to bring them into direct communication with any official would have been open to many objections. Confusions might arise when visitors were absent; new visitors would occasionally have to be appointed, and to have their work explained to them. No relieving officer would have time to undertake this duty, nor even to communicate with so large and fluctuating a body as that formed by these volunteers. The Guardians, therefore, resolved to recognize one of these volunteers as representing the whole body. The referee would be a connecting link between themselves and the visitors, and through her only, all communications would pass. I was asked to fill this position with relation to the Guardians, for one reason, because I was already a member both of the Relief Committee before mentioned, and the committee of the Charity Organization Society, and the recognized medium of communication between these two bodies.

After the combination of volunteer and official agency had thus been arranged, which was in the winter of 1872-3, the Guardians directed the relieving officer who is in charge of the St. Mary's Poor Law District, to send me daily a list containing the name of each applicant from that district, with his address, ages of family, and nature of application.[1] I send out the information at once to the visitor in whose court the applicant resides, with a blank form[2] on which she may report any facts bearing on the character and circumstances of the family, which appear to her to be such as the Poor Law authorities ought to know. She can report by giving a summary of the information contained in her district-book, and return the form at once, or she can re-visit the applicant and give later information in addition if she deems it necessary. She sends her report to me, and I forward it to the relieving officer, who uses it as he may see fit. In many instances it gives information which the relieving officer might not otherwise possess, as, for instance, that an applicant is in receipt of money paid by the visitor, or known by her to be paid by local charity. In other cases the report gives clues for further investigation by him, as where it mentions the existence of grown-up sons and daughters who may be able to give help.[3] After the weekly meeting of the board, I am informed of the decision arrived at in each case, by a list sent to me similar to that furnished to every Guardian. These particulars I send to the visitors of the courts where applicants reside, and they are entered in the several district-books. The average number of applicants in the Poor Law District of St. Mary's is forty-five weekly, and the number of visitors engaged in the work is thirty-five. The number of visitors has doubled during the last year, so that we have subdivided all the larger courts and streets. Additional clergymen are coming into active co-operation with us, and some few gentlemen have come forward to act as visitors. These may all be considered hopeful signs that the movement is gaining ground.

It will be seen from this outline, that in St. Mary's district there are four agencies employed in the endeavor to administer relief to the necessitous in the wisest and most really helpful way: the Guardians, with their relieving officer, the Charity Organization Society, the Relief Committee, and the District Visitors. These four agencies are connected and brought into efficient co-operation by the referee, who directs and superintends the visitors, attends the meetings of the Charity Organization Society, and of the Relief Committee, and is the medium through which the Board of Guardians acquire information otherwise inaccessible to them.

The immediate direct effect of the adoption of this system upon the Poor Law cases may be slight; it may be that the information supplied by the district visitors does not in many instances modify the decisions of the Board; but this is the least part of the work. If the visitors really learn their duties, and apprehend the spirit of the system they have undertaken to carry out, it is impossible to measure the effect which the work may have in diminishing pauperism and inducing more provident habits of life among our laboring classes; and thus, along with other advantages, reducing the heavy burden of the poor-rates. The connection with the Poor Law system is calculated to be of great advantage to the visitors. They will learn something of its working; they will be enabled to use with much greater effect and with much greater frequency the lever which distaste for the "House" puts into their hands; and knowing that while the workhouse exists even the idle and improvident and reckless need not starve, they will be encouraged to refuse to such persons the pauperizing doles of a merely impulsive charity, in the belief that such refusal will probably benefit the individual, and will certainly in the long run benefit the class.

The plan described resembles the one in operation at Elberfeld, inasmuch as it is based on the same principle; sub-division of work among a large number of volunteer visitors, grouped under recognized though unpaid leaders. As in Elberfeld, we have not sought to enlist visitors who can give their whole time to the work. We want those living in their own homes, surrounded by their own interests and connections, and who can bring individual sympathy and thought to bear on a very few families. A large number of visitors are needed, and we could not obtain them if those only were eligible who could give a large amount of time to the work. Even more intimate knowledge of individual families is secured in Marylebone than we have any evidence of in the case of Elberfeld, because here in their own small districts the visitors undertake duties for other bodies as well as for the Guardians. Our volunteers are constantly in the courts, on business connected with the local charities, with the Charity Organization Society, and also with the School Board: and though I must not here enlarge on the particular form of their work for these different bodies, I may point out that the entire truth is better elicited by those who come into communication with the poor in various ways: facts concealed from them in one capacity being revealed to them in another. For example, the desire on the part of parents to represent the ages of children to the Poor Law visitor as young enough to receive parochial relief, is counteracted by their desire to represent them to the school board visitor as old enough to exempt them from attendance at school.

The important difference between the Elberfeld and Marylebone systems is that, whereas in Elberfeld the volunteers themselves decide on the parochial relief, our volunteers have no such authority committed to them. It would be a fundamental change of the gravest nature to throw any share of such responsibility on the visitor, and would be a change not only disastrous, until the visitors have more experience, but in my opinion probably unadvisable even in the future. The large discretionary power exercised by Guardians under our English Poor Law (which contrasts with the very definite scale for out-door relief in use at Elberfeld) would make it an additional difficulty to place the decisions as to grants in the hands of visitors. In fact, in every case, so that only the evidence brought before him be sufficient, it is easier for a judge or arbitrator to deal in a uniform manner with cases which come before him when he is not brought into close communication with those whom his decision affects. So that the division of duty in Marylebone, where the visitor brings information and the Guardians vote relief, appears to be the right one. It is, moreover, a real help to the visitor in maintaining a satisfactory footing among the people under her charge, for them to know that, though she will listen to and represent their claims for relief, the absolute award of it does not rest with her.

I may perhaps here point out that there is one small addition to the system, which, though it would be of no direct advantage to the Poor Law authorities, would be of great service to those who are administering the local charities. I have already mentioned that the Guardians send to me as referee an official weekly report of the cases decided by them; but the grounds of their decision are not given, and often they may be such as would, if known to us, influence grants from the charities. If the Guardians saw no objection to allowing one or two representative volunteers to be present at their weekly meetings, this information would reach us fully and regularly. It would also afford guidance to the visitors if we could know to what extent the information furnished by them to the relieving officer is received and acted upon.

There is one further addition to the scheme which has been suggested. It has been said that it might be well to empower the volunteers to pay the regular out-door relief of the aged at their own homes, instead of compelling them, as at present, to gather at the workhouse door to receive it. As to the advantages of this plan I have as yet come to no decision. On the one hand, it is a gain that the poor should not be obliged to congregate for relief, which has a pauperizing effect upon them; and moreover the weekly visitation of the home would form a regular method of inspection. On the other hand, as I have stated above, the less the visitor is contemplated as an almoner, the more independent and satisfactory are her relations likely to be with her people,—and I fear the distinction between bringing and giving relief would not be very clear to recipients.

In conclusion, I may say that the system described above, would, when perfectly carried out, ensure that out-door relief should be confined to the deserving, and that drunken and idle people should be offered the workhouse only. Thus far our volunteer workers are fully aware of the objects for which they are associated together. But I am myself satisfied that the scheme is capable of a far deeper influence on the condition of the poor, when the volunteers shall rise to the perception that, in dealing with poverty, they must aim at prevention rather than at cure; at saving those under their influence from sinking to the Poor-law Level, rather than merely obtaining relief for them when they have reached that low point. Few of my fellow-workers have as yet grasped the idea that their best success would be to develop the resources of the poor themselves, instead of letting them come upon the rates, or continue upon them. I think they rarely set before themselves the desire to find some employment, at hand or far off, which may support the young widow and her children before she has tasted parish bread. I think they rarely press upon the old woman the duty of first trying if the successful son cannot support her, or the daughters in service unite to do so. They have not yet watched the poor closely enough to see that this would be in reality the truest kindness. They forget the dignity of self-maintenance, they forget the blessing of drawing the bonds of relationship closer, and dwell only upon the fact that the applicant is deserving—see only the comfort or relief which the parish allowance would secure.

How far they can raise the people by degrees above the degrading need of charitable or Poor Law relief, to be energetic, self-reliant, provident, and industrious, will depend upon the height of their own hope, the patience of their own labor, the moral courage which will teach them to prefer being helpful to being popular, and finally to the temper and spirit of their own homes and lives. For, say what we may, if our upper class were to become extravagant, improvident, and showy, it would be aped by those below it, even though as surely it would be despised. And if we desire to be the leaders of our poor into the ways of happy prosperity, we must order our homes in exactly the same spirit as theirs must be ordered, in simplicity, industry, and providence.

I have, etc.

OCTAVIA HILL.

To the Right Honorable
James Stansfeld, M. P.

-

1. A copy of the form is appended to this letter.
2. A copy of this form filled in with a specimen report is also appended.
3. To prevent serious consequences in urgent cases, the relieving officer is authorized to give relief without awating the visitor's report. He is also bound to verify any statements which appear to require it. His responsibility to the Board is thus not weakened, while the information upon which he acts is more complete. Even when the information does not reach him until after temporary relief has been administered, it is still valuable for his future guidance.

Printed in Great Britain
by Amazon